Monograph 63
THE AMERICAN ETHNOLOGICAL SOCIETY
Robert F. Spencer, *Editor*

*

SANTA EULALIA'S PEOPLE:

Ritual Structure and Process
in an Andalucian Multicommunity

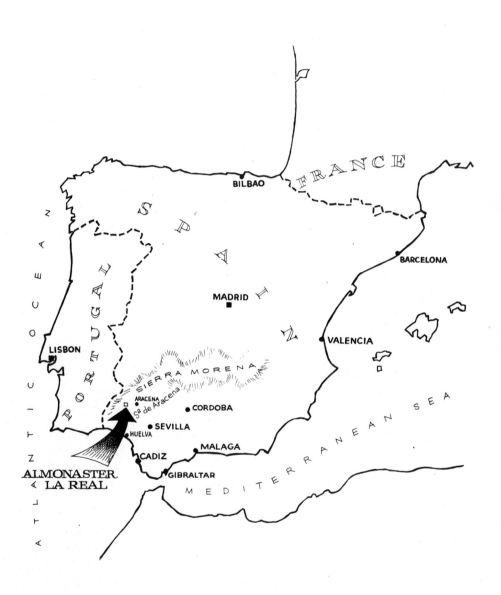

SANTA EULALIA'S PEOPLE:

Ritual Structure and Process
in an Andalucian Multicommunity

Francisco Enrique Aguilera

WEST PUBLISHING CO.
St. Paul • New York
Los Angeles • San Francisco

COPYRIGHT © 1978 By WEST PUBLISHING CO.
          50 West Kellogg Boulevard
          P.O. Box 3526
          St. Paul, Minnesota 55165

Printed in the United States of America

Library of Congress Cataloging in Publication Data

Aguilera, Francisco Enrique
    Santa Eulalia's people.
    (Monograph—The American Ethnological Society; no. 63)
    Bibliography: p.
    Includes index.
    1. Festivals—Spain—Almonaster la Real.
    2. Almonaster la Real, Spain—Social life and customs.
    3. Almonaster la Real, Spain—Religious life and customs.
    4. Central places—Spain. I. Title. II. Series: American Ethnological Society. Monographs; no. 63.
GT4862.A64A38   390'.0946'87   77-26272
ISBN 0-8299-0164-7

Preface

This book is the outgrowth of one part of my doctoral dissertation. That study was the result of almost two years of continuous residence and study in the Término of Almonaster La Real, Province of Huelva, Spain. From 1967 to 1969 my wife Barbara and I shared the life of town and villages. The people of Almonaster knew what we were doing and were extremely helpful, their one request was that we recreate as truly as possible the culture and society of their home. It is by their request that I have used the true name and location of Almonaster in my writings.[1]

My training at the University of Pennsylvania was as a Latin Americanist and the original fieldwork proposal presented to the Department of Anthropology had several goals. I hoped not only to add to the growing literature on Spain but also to develop useful comparative data for the study of Latin American communities. What I called a "Spanish reference point" for the study of Latin American communities was really a social-structural model. It was supposed to emerge from the comparison of two field studies. Two rural agrarian areas were picked, one in Spain and one in Colombia, S.A. After a year of studying intra- and intercommunity social organization in Spain we planned to go to Colombia and repeat the study. In spite of the several hundred years of separate history, we hoped that the comparison would yield valuable insights into the Spanish component of Latin American communities.

The richness of the daily and ritual culture of Almonaster, with all it had to offer for the theory of community and multicommunity, effectively postponed the South American study. We stayed in Spain for the entire field period.

Within three weeks of our arrival in Spain we had found and settled into Almonaster. The speed and ease with which we reached this decision is owed, in great degree, to the generosity and friendship of Alfredo

Jiménez Nuñéz, Decano and Catedrático of Anthropology at the University of Sevilla. Don Alfredo not only opened the Department of Anthropology to us but also dedicated his time to helping us survey the area where we hoped to find our research site. Another important factor in our speedy choice was the character of the people of Almonaster. From the first we were overwhelmed by their warmth and interest and aid, which continued throughout our stay. All of these friends can't be mentioned but in particular we must mention Don Isidoro Palomo Martín, Alcalde of Almonaster la Real, whose generosity in all things made our research possible; also Don Francisco Arroyo Cotán-Pinto, chief doctor of the Término; Don Isaías Delgado García, head of the Patrimonio Forestal; Don José García Romero; Don Francisco Barrero Delgado; Don Ricardo Sánchez Infantes; Don Juan José Vázquez Márquez; Don Damian Sánchez Lopez. For lack of space we cannot continue to list all to whom we owe so much, but to Srta. Rosario and Señora Concepción Vázquez Barrero of the Pensión Santa Eualia, who took special care to advise us on the ways of Almonaster; and to Srtas. María de Gracia Romero Sánchez and Dolores Vázquez Ignacio, who have continued to send us data since leaving the field, we owe a special debt.

An important acknowledgment is to the silent partner of the research team, Barbara Harris Aguilera, who not only aided in all phases of the fieldwork but also acted as my constant editor and critic.

Throughout my graduate and undergraduate career at the University of Pennsylvania I amassed many debts to the faculty. The most important acknowledgment is to Dr. Rubén E. Reina, who was the most insistent, constantly forcing me to think but never telling me what to think. As the supervisor of my doctoral research, his friendship and advice were indispensable. In the writing of my dissertation I am indebted to Drs. Ward H. Goodenough and Robert McC. Netting for their comments, criticisms, and moral support. To Dr. Thomas C. Greaves goes the credit for suggesting that I read Gregory Bateson's work on schismogenesis. All of these men are among the most responsible for my training but I, of course, accept the full responsibility for the implementation of that training in this study.

The actual fieldwork was carried out from December 1967 to August 1969 while I was an NDEA Title IV Fellow. My travel to and from Spain was made possible by grants from the Department of Anthropology of the University of Pennsylvania.

In the writing of this book I created more debts. In addition to those previously listed I must include Dr. Robert F. Spencer, editor of this series. Our correspondence began in 1974 and his excellent criticism both in the rejection of an earlier manuscript and the acceptance of this one was invaluable. At Boston University I have spent the last years subjecting the ideas in this book to the critical eye of several dozen students. I can not list them here but they have had a much greater hand in this book than they were ever aware of at the time. Dr. Reina and my wife continued as valued editors and critics and to their company I must add Dr. Hamish Gillies whose literary scalpel and diagnosis have added immeasurably to the quality of this book. Again, of course, the help was theirs, but the responsibility is mine. Thanks are also due to Mrs. Bertha Mintz and Ms. Silvie Olney who typed the present manuscript.

During the field period I was aided by the visit of my father, Enrique Aguilera, an astute observer whose knowledge of the technology and culture of rural Colombia gave new meaning to the data being collected. My mother Marian Aguilera and my grandmother Jennie R. Dornblum read and edited the original manuscript. The gratitude to my family is not simply based on kinship but on the very real debt which I owe to each for their part in this study.

This book is for the people of Almonaster: in memory of Mr. Robert Riggs; and, dedicated to Barbara Harris Aguilera.

NOTES

[1]It should be noted throughout that this book is set in the late 1960s and early seventies. The manuscript was essentially completed in early 1976. Generalizations about Spanish government and the wider social setting in which Almonaster is found are meant to reflect only the situation at the time of the study. Post-Fanco Spain, with its many dramatic economic and governmental changes, is not a part of this narrative.

*

Contents

*

SANTA EULALIA'S PEOPLE:

**Ritual Structure and Process
in an Andalucian Multicommunity**

ERMITA DE ALMONASTER
ALZADO ESTE.

CHAPTER 1

Introduction

This is a book about life in a rural corner of Spain, a book about ritual, and about the shared social organization of sixteen small villages and one small town. But it is not the standard ethnographic survey of a region, for the town and villages are not isolated from each other but share in a higher level of social organization called a multicommunity (Reina 1965). The life of each settlement might be described separately but full understanding of any one of them can only come through consideration of the entire system of communities. Multicommunities are inventions of necessity, they exist because each component community would be unable to survive on its own, because the individual community is too small, lacking in social, cultural, and economic resources. But the multicommunity is more than a convenient relationship between groups of people. It is an affective universe, full of sentiment and meaning, which far transcends the daily problems of individual survival. The multicommunity is a distinctive cultural entity, made up of the agreement between the distinctive cultures of each of its component communities. It is also a conscious identity, made up of the distinctive identities of its member groups.

This multicommunity takes its name from the central town, Almonaster. This book is about the central theme of Almonaster's social organization, its ritual life.

1

THE MODEL OF COMMUNITY AND MULTICOMMUNITY

"What is Almonaster and how does it work?" was the question which sent us to Spain in the first place, although in the planning stage I asked, "What is community social organization and how does it work?" At first this seemed a silly question since concepts of community have long existed in anthropology. Certainly, a standard short definition, which most anthropologists would find familiar, can be easily phrased. Community social organization is a territorially based social grouping in which membership is conferred through residence in the territory and within whose boundaries there is consensus or cultural sharing with regard to the specific form that internal society should take and which presents certain "collective representations" to the outside world. But deeper review of the anthropologists' use of the concept shows that further elaboration of this short definition has lead each anthropologist in a different direction and into basic disagreement. Full definitions vary greatly. There is a basic uncertainty in anthropological usage as to just what "community" means. Is it truly a form of social organization, or is it, after all, just a way of collecting data? Is it both a type of social organization and a method, or is it, in fact, neither? Is it simply an idea which became so real to anthropologists that they began to see it in the lives of the people they studied when it really wasn't there? And, finally, even if it is a type of social organization does it explain the important modern questions of how local society is integrated with, influenced by, and contributes to wider national and regional social and cultural systems?

Community

In recent years only a few authors have successfully attempted to define in any detail the structure of the social organization type called community. The two most influential works are by Wolf (1955) and Arensberg (1961). Each has approached the subject from a different direction and each has contributed to my own model.

In a landmark article (1955), Eric Wolf advanced the concept of the "closed corporate community." He emphasized the corporate control of material resources but implicit in his definition is a degree of sociological corporateness as well.

> The distinctive characteristic of the corporate peasant community is that it represents a bounded social system with clear-cut limits, in relations to

both outsiders and insiders. It has structural identity over time. Seen from the outside, the community as a whole carries on a series of activities and upholds certain "collective representations." Seen from within it defines the rights and duties of its members and prescribes large segments of their behavior (1955, p. 456).

In the corporate peasant community, the relationships of individuals and kin groups within the community are bounded by a common structure. We have seen that the community aims primarily at maintaining an equilibrium of roles within the community in an effort to keep intact its outer boundary. Maintenance of the outer boundary reacts in turn on the stability of the equilibrium within it (1955:463).

The article goes on to describe a contrasting community type called the "open community." Unfortunately this second definition lacks the impact of the closed corporate one since the open community is largely defined as being the opposite of the closed one. Thus Wolf's "open" type is in part defined by the lack of "such a formalized corporate structure. It neither limits its membership nor insists on a defensive boundary. Quite the contrary, it permits free permeation by outside influences" (1955:463). It is the insistence on the idea of corporateness as the means to a "defensive boundary" that handicaps both community definitions. For the closed community it creates undue emphasis on the maintenance of internal equilibrium. In the open community this emphasis on the defensive aspects of corporateness forces Wolf to the logical (not necessarily empirically based) conclusion that openness of boundaries and the absence of corporate control of natural resources precludes any meaningful level of sociological corporateness. He is thus unable to define open community in terms of the degree to which it is a corporate social entity; that is, he is unable to use the same general model to generate both types of community.

If we recognize, however, that corporate control by any group may range from the concrete level of physical resources through the metaphysical level of control over styles and patterns of behavior to the level of group identity,[1] then we must assume that all units of social organization are corporate to some degree. Following the logic of the closed corporate definition we might say that "community" functions, in reaction to both internal and external pressures, to produce a "structured field of inter-individual relationships" (Arensberg 1961:250), creating an equilibrium and degree of corporateness roughly equal to the extent to which the structured field is bounded by the community. We have now phrased an equation which may usefully be applied to any type of community. The ideas of equilibrium and corporateness as community goals are key to this equation. The equilibrium in this case is a dynamic one, and means a friction-free movement of the system, what Wallace (1956) has called a "steady state." This does not preclude change or evolution within the community but indicates that such change must be slow and functionally integrated into the cultural system in order to keep the equilibrium intact. Corporateness is the result of the group's ability to maintain structural equilibrium by, at least, attempting to exert group control over all areas of culture. These attempts will only be partially successful in any specific environment and so corporateness will vary as to degree from case to case.

So far we have the development of a characterization of community process but are still far from an explicit structural definition of community itself. Here it is necessary to turn to the work of Arensberg, whose 1961 formulation is an excellent beginning. In "Community as Object and as Sample," Arensberg had two goals in mind. First, he tried to define community as the point at which society and culture are isomorphic; that is, community as a type of social organization. Second, he was attempting to demonstrate that once properly defined and selected, the community was a valid sample from which to make generalizations about the national culture and society of which the community is a part. The impossibility of this second goal had a deleterious effect on the structural definition he advanced to meet the first goal. His definition is an operational one employing four factors:

> first, personnel—a minimum table of organization of two sexes and three generations, and patterns of interaction among those filling all social roles: second, space—a settlement pattern: third, time—a continuity of roles through generations on the one hand and, on the other, rhythms and periodicities of movement and activities: fourth, culture—behavior that must include either the actual existence of, or knowledge of, at least the minimum number of roles that distinguish the culture (Friedl 1966:1022).

By including culture Arensberg seems to be catering to his goal of community as the perfect sample. The culture factor seems out of place as being of a higher order than the other three, it is both the major unknown and the major factor in the definition of the first three factors. That is, culture is both the product of and the precondition for the ongoing existence of the first three factors. In a purely operational sense, it seems clear that only after gaining an understanding of the mechanisms and culture specific definitions of every other aspect of such a structural definition can one have an understanding of the "minimum number of roles that distinguish the culture" of the local society, let alone the larger society of which it is a part.

Excluding "culture," we see that Arensberg has framed a definition which does not violate the less formal statements of Wolf, but which still does not speak to the central process of community which is the truest product of Wolf's work. Thus keeping in mind the statement about process derived from Wolf, I would add three new factors to Arensberg's elements of *personnel, time,* and *space*. The resulting model is one that may be applied to any social organization type. The universality of this model is created by carefully maintaining all of its features at the same level of abstraction. In addition to Arensberg's factors of personnel, time, and space, the finished model includes *principle of recruitment, principle of group maintenance,* and *principles of interpersonal network formation*. The first of these added features allows for the universality of the model. In the case of community the principle of recruitment is given as "residence;" if the model were to be used for descent systems of social organization, then this one feature would be given as "kinship."

The second of the added features, the principle of group maintenance, acknowledges the existence of some means for collective group identity maintenance and formation within the community. That is, "community" includes a process by which collective representations are generated by which the organism is known to the outside and by which it identifies *itself* as a distinct, definable, sociocultural entity. This process of self-identification is partly achieved by the reification of basic social and cultural definitions (often through ritual). In addition, as this process seems to be so commonly structured in a system of segmental oppositions (cf., Bateson 1958; Fortes 1953; Murdock 1949) which are characterized by group competition and/or cooperation, the working of this principle also functions to maintain harmony within the system by releasing and channeling dysfunctional interpersonal tension toward positive group-oriented goals and reification of the cultural order.[2]

The principles of interpersonal network formation, function to provide the basic integrating mechanisms within the community society. Through the channels of communication which they set up, these principles ensure a minimum degree of cultural homogeneity within the system. As such, the principles of interpersonal network formation are seen as the culture's inventory of values, beliefs, and patterns for generating dyadic relationships between roles. With this in mind, it becomes obvious that they are not to be confused with ego-based personal networks. In the former case, the individual is seen as a participant in several patterns of network; in the latter case, each person would be seen as the center of a constellation of linked individuals.

Not only does this six part model lend itself to a more careful and systematic characterization of community and to expansion to cover higher level sociocultural entities, but it also serves the more important function of removing the geographic determinism which has traditionally been a covert characteristic of community models. By distinguishing between the principles of recruitment (residence) and the principle of group maintenance, it becomes possible to outline a set of community dynamics which rises above the simplistic notion that the people are a sociocultural group because of spatial propinquinty.

Before turning to multicommunity, an expansion of the community model, it is important to note that this is not an "ideal" model, impossiable to find in nature, but an optimal one, not unknown in the ethnographic record. Almonaster is an optimal example of the community model. Community sociocultural "health" depends on the delicate balance between all of the community factors. In the real world the function of each factor must be counter-balanced by the functioning of the rest. In many, perhaps most, Spanish rural communities this balance has been upset, leading to dramatic change at best and, at worst, to the extinction of particular communities and their distinctive cultures. In Almonaster the collective, annual ritual cycle is still able to balance the system.

Multicommunity

Definitions of multicommunity are rare, rarer even than good definitions of community. This is due, in part, to the fact that the study of multicommunity often involves working in a setting which includes a larger, less peasant (in economic terms) and more "open" community—traditionally not the choice of most anthropologists—along with several more "peasant" ones. The result is a several community research focus which is also fairly uncommon among anthropologists. In their article of 1955, Wagley and Harris skirt the edges of the concept with their "town type" Latin American subculture, but this mention is a cursory one which appears never to have been followed up in detail.

The term "multicommunity" itself was coined by Reina (1965) and is used by him in a descriptive manner rather than as the subject of an explicit, generalized structural definition. Nevertheless, it is interesting to note that he too begins with the Wolf typology (1955). In his description of the Peten of Guatemala, Reina records a group of settlements "which are closer to the open-type community" (Wolf, 1955:461–466; Reina 1965:362–363). These "open" communities have been forced to develop "a social organization of intercommunity relation," a "total system of articulation among inter-related communities," which he labels a multi-community (1965:389). Interestingly, this is due to the degree of corporateness manifested by each of these "open" communities. Reina writes:

> as each Peten town perpetuates its own identity to the degree described in this paper, cultural merging becomes difficult. Therefore, from a practical viewpoint, Peteneros realize the need to coordinate their efforts in some areas of daily activities, and communication among them is very complete in as much as they share much of the cultural content (1965:388).

This example mirrors the use of "corporateness" in my own community model as it demonstrates that the corporate drive of "open" communities in a multicommunity setting is a powerful force. Rather than tend toward decreased corporateness due to its openess and its interaction with other like units, the open community will in this case have an increased tendency in the direction of corporateness. In the multicommunity setting, to paraphrase Fortes (1953 in Ottenberg 1960:174), "What marks a community (lineage) out and maintains its identity . . . , is the fact that it emerges most precisely in a complementary relationship with or in opposition to like units."

In analytical terms the multicommunity is simply an extension of the community form of social organization to a higher level of sociocultural integration. It is an adaptation by several communities to the complex national and regional environment in which they find themselves. This collectivity of communities, because of its greater demographic and physical size and its greater diversity, is more able to cope with economic, political, social, and religious conditions than any single component community. Although the individual community must relinquish control over some of its basic dimensions, the adaptation insures it of a reasonable degree of autonomy and corporate control over the rest of its basic institutions.

While all six components of the model can be found at the multicommunity level, the two which seem most sociologically significant are the group principle and the network principles. In terms of the former, it is clear that the multicommunity represents a bounded universe of community competitors for the functioning of the group principle of each of the component communities, while at the same time it represents the field upon which a higher inter-community collective identity and structure is maintained. In terms of the latter, the network principles, it is clear that at the multicommunity level the inter-community networks which they generate are patterns or mechanisms which facilitate the flow of resources within the collectivity of communities. They also facilitate the maintenance of some degree of cultural sharing or homogeneity between member communities. Such networks, of course, extend far beyond the multicommunity itself, but their frequency, duration, and intensity drop precipitously at the multicommunity boundary. Though they do continue in attenuated state, they will not contravene the corporate stance of the multicommunity in its relations with its neighbors and the nation as a whole. Still it is important to remember that the multicommunity may be said to be corporate only to the degree to which the field of interpersonal relations is contained by the multicommunity boundary.

THE MODEL IN ETHNOGRAPHIC PRACTICE

It is one thing to construct a model, but another to put it into practice as an analytical tool. In practice the older models all suffered from the same flaw, lack of attention to the definition and description of the community boundaries. Ethnographies have been written which assert the importance of boundaries but which simply appear to assume or impose them in an a priori fashion. In ethnographic practice there is usually an implicit assumption that the physical boundary of a small town or village is the social and cultural boundary of the "community." In their theories some like Wolf have stressed the importance of community social and cultural boundaries, but "community scholars" do not usually bother to theorize on the extension or maintenance of these boundaries. Thus the function of boundaries is stressed, but the process which creates them and maintains them is left unstated. A theory which does not deal with these aspects of structure and process will always be found wanting in ethnographic application. In my own model, attention to group and network principles seeks to explain and define the boundaries of the community, rather than simply accept them. This is the key to a better understanding of the community. It is the only way to be certain that one has in fact seen all of the community. The structural elements of the community model are abstractions; in reality they are found in a much more complex organizational form. In the case of group and network principles two forms of community boundary are a complex manifestation of the abstract structural principles.

The principle of group formation and maintenance generates *boundaries of sentiment*. By boundaries of sentiment, I mean the boundaries of corporately held group identities. Here the boundary is absolute, a symbolic value. A person either shares in the identity and is within it or does not share and is without it. A person may share in a variety of identities at a variety of sociocultural levels, but in the application of the community model, I am only interested in those identities which coincide with a bounded society and which are the results of the sharing of a distinctive culture. Thus, one cannot say or feel that they share a certain identity, they must also demonstrate their membership by behavior which illustrates their correct participation in local society and their implicit sharing of local culture. Boundaries of sentiment therefore enclose self-conscious groups.

The extent to which the boundary of sentiment encloses a bounded community or multicommunity society may be assessed by scrutiny of a second set of boundaries—*boundaries of instrumentality*. These are the statistically defined boundaries of the network of interpersonal relations. I use the word "instrumentality" to underline the fact that the pattern of network interaction generated by the network principles are put to use by individual social actors to achieve conscious or unconscious instrumental goals. They are the ways people "get things done." The boundary of instrumentality is that point in social and physical space where duration, frequency, and density of contact falls off precipitiously. In this sense the boundary is statistically defined. For example, Latin American and European communities are often characterized as endogamous; that is, the kinship networks which are created by marriage are said to be bounded by the community, since, following a rule of endogamy, one has to select a mate from one's own social group. But the boundary of this particular network cannot be said to be absolute, since there is always some minimal number of spouses who are drawn from outside the community. The boundary is not absolute, but it does present a case of severe restriction at some point in space. If most or all networks are restricted at the same social and/or physical point, we begin to see a pattern of social intercourse in which there is a great deal of communication on the "inside" and much, much less crossing the boundary to the "outside." This point of severe restriction is the boundary of instrumentality and, in the case of most communities and multicommunities, that boundary tends to coincide rather nicely with the boundaries of sentiment of those units.

In this book only one element of the community model will be central, the *group principle*. The full ethnographic description of all of the several elements of the community model would be much too long for one book. Consequently, in this first book on Almonaster I have chosen the topic of ritual because it will supply the fullest body of data from which to examine the structure, function, and process of the group principles which underlie the boundaries of sentiment. For it is only in the exposition of the group principle at the community and multicommunity levels that I can make the best case for the existence of both community and multicommunity social organization.

THE ROAD TO ALMONASTER

Ethnography is the product of the interaction of two realities experienced by the ethnographer. One is a theoretical reality internalized through years of study in libraries and classrooms; the other is a social reality experienced in the field. In this case the social reality began on the road to Almonaster.

In the southwestern corner of Spain lies the province of Huelva. The Sierra de Aracena, as the mountainous northern part of the province is known, is a region of rural towns and villages isolated from each other and from the outside world among the hills. Only two main roads cross this region. One road from the south connects the city of Huelva with the cities of the province of Extremadura in the north. The other comes from the southeast and runs along the mountains between Sevilla and the Portuguese border. In the center of the mountains a small, narow road leaves the Sevilla road and runs parallel to it behind a wall of mountains, only to return to the same highway twenty miles to the west. Almonaster La Real, the central town in this study, is the largest of four towns on this narrow and forgotten road.

The Sevilla road begins on the banks of the Guadalquivir River, just to the west of the city of Sevilla. Here it is a modern highway, which cuts across the rolling plains of the river. The area is under intensive mechanized cultivation. The fields stretch in gentle waves to the horizon. But once in the foothills of the Sierra Morena, the agriculture changes and the fields are smaller. At the provincial line between Sevilla and Huelva the highway branches. One branch goes to the north but the road to Almonaster is along the west branch which continues to Aracena and beyond to Portugal. At the entrance to Aracena, an important town, the judicial center for all the northern Huelvan towns, the narrow road to

Almonaster begins. By now the mechanized fields of Sevilla are far behind and both minifundia and latifundia of a more traditional nature are the rule. Unlike the flat lands, the Sierra is covered with trees; all are carefully tended. These are not forests but orchards and tree-filled pastures. Olives and other fruit trees are plentiful as are domestic oaks, including the *alcornoque* which yields cork, and the *encina*, whose large sweet acorns are an important fodder. Still the countryside seems wild and lonely.

The road clings to the side of the steep hills, passing through stands of encina and pine. Were it not for the neat stone walls and the occasional farmer with his mule or donkey walking by the side of the road, the place would seem uninhabited. Those familiar with the region know that there are extensive cultivated fields hidden below the road in the valleys, but the visitor's first impressions are of silent mountains. Coming around a bend and over a rise one sees, through the encinas, the spire of a church. This is the landmark of a town. Soon the burnt orange tile roofs of the town come into view clustered around the church. Finally the road dips down to meet the edge of town, and the illusion of its being a tiny miniature is broken. The houses at the edge of town are whitewashed; further in, the larger houses of the rich may have stone facades, but they too are whitewashed. The church, always the largest building, is of blue gray shale with a carved portal of limestone. The center of town is dominated by a large, two or three story, building which is the *ayuntamiento* or town hall.

Almonaster is like its neighbors with a few unique exceptions. The first sight of the town is not the church spire, but the tower of the Moorish castle which sits on a hill above the town. The town lies in a saddle between the castle and the mountain, San Cristóbal, rising over a thousand feet above the town to reach a height of over three thousand feet. The mountain is the highest in the area and one can see nearly a hundred miles to the ocean from its heights.

Turning into the town from the road, one enters the first small plaza which opens to the church. The church is larger than those of the other towns on the road. It is famous for its "Manuelino portal," a beautifully worked doorway in the Portuguese style of the late fifteenth century. Further into the town, past balconies overflowing with geraniums and windows with elaborate metal gratings, is the main plaza with its orange trees and central fountain. Surrounding the plaza are the houses of old rich families and the *ayuntamiento*, whitewashed in white with yellow trim.

The towns along the road are officially classified as *villas*, "towns," which are each the seat of government of a *término municipal*. The término municipal, commonly called a *término*, is a large expanse of territory analogous to a county. The population governed from the ayuntamiento includes all of the town dwellers, in the case of Almonaster almost eight hundred people, and the people living scattered throughout the término. For Almonaster this means another 3,900 people. Few of these people actually live dispersed about the countryside. Some live at the mining camps in the southern part of the término;[3] but most live in small village communities called *aldeas* which vary in size from a handful of small, whitewashed houses to a large and prosperous village with a chapel and even a store or two. Each of the fourteen aldeas has a name, and the entire término is known by the name of the town, Almonaster La Real.[4] In addition there are two aldea-like communities at the two railroad stations on the line which passes through the término.

UNKNOWN ALMONASTER

At the beginning of fieldwork one must grapple with the unknown. In an unknown culture and society it may take weeks or months to formulate in the new cultural idiom of the field site the theoretical questions brought from home. In this early period, simple questions at the ethnographic level help the researcher to find his social and cultural bearings. The questions which are most compelling are those which are generated by the apparently paradoxical behavior, beliefs, or values of one's new friends. In time, with greater understanding of the local sociocultural system, most of these questions are easily resolved and cease to be important; a few, however, remain as striking indications of the structure and process of local culture and society. The following are three such apparent paradoxes from Almonaster. The first apparent paradox is obvious during one's first visit to the town. Although Almonaster shares with other towns of the region in the broad parameters of environment and economy, the personality of Almonaster emerges in sharp contrast with its neighbors. Notable is the candor, warmth, and apparent self-confidence with which the people greet the outsider. In many adjacent parts of the region people seem depressed. In many places, the internal poverty of the mountain regions has taken from the people the clean, healthy, and proud life, which the poor of Almonaster still manifest. The question becomes, "What is it about Almonaster which has enabled Almuñenses to hold onto the 'good life,' inspite of material conditions, while so many around them seem to have lost so much?"[5]

After closer contact with Almonaster, a second paradox emerges. People express two, apparently contradictory, views of their society. On the one hand, they stress the sociological corporateness and egalitarian character of local society; while, on the other hand, they point out the importance of the clearly defined social and economic hierarchy of their society. This stratification is not unobtrusive, for the economic differences and their associated social markings are clearly drawn. The rich of Almonaster would be considered rich even by the standards of the United States, with their Mercedes automobiles and large and economically productive land holdings in other parts of Spain and Portugal. In contrast, the poor of Almonaster do not spatially segregate themselves. The richest mansions often share a party wall with the most humble farmer's low-ceilinged home. Nor can anyone in this rural agrarian setting ignore the fact that the poor depend on the rich for much of their access to agricultural land and part-time jobs. To the Almuñense the community is "like a family, interdependent, responsible for each other," it is a place where "all men are equal," at the same time it is a place where some are rich or educated and deserving of "respect" and deference, a place where all are aware of the ranked hierarchy and of their position within it and their dependence upon it. The question may be phrased, "How does local culture and society maintain two opposing points of view, inspite of a 'pragmatic' economic reality which should daily reinforce only one of these points of view, in time, eliminating egalitarianism in favor of hierarchicalism?"

Closely associated with this second paradox is a final one. Almuñenses recognize one paramount value for all adults, *formalidad*, one of whose basic tenets is the total proscription of all expression of overt hostility. There are no angry shouts, scuffles, physical violence, offenses to property, or even stumbling drunks on the streets of Almonaster. What happens to the tensions of interpersonal hostility which, logic predicts, must be engendered by the movement of individuals through life and social organization, but which by cultural definition may not be expressed and which in social practice is not expressed?

Each of these initial questions was resolved in the end, and in each solution the function and structure of the group principle was central. I will return to them in the conclusion, but here I must warn the reader that this book cannot pretend to detail the full complexity of their causes, or even of their effect, during much of yearly life for they are drawn from the full range of the social and cultural complexity of

Almonaster. The following is an account of Almonaster which is stripped to the ethnographic bone. In the first section, which describes the rites of passage of the life cycle, I will sketch in the primary components of the shared culture of the multicommunity. Here I can describe basic values and beliefs and some of the roles and patterns of behavior which characterize Almonaster. The complexity of the inventory of roles and statuses, economic strategy and network, or cultural ecology are beyond the scope of this first book on Almonaster.[6] In succeeding sections, on the rites of intensification of the annual cycle, I will show how these complex rituals reify and mediate these basic cultural and social understandings and how through this process they intensify and maintain the corporate group identities which characterize the multicommunity of Almonaster and its individual component communities. I hope to let Almonaster speak for itself, keeping theoretical statements at a minimum until the conclusion.

NOTES

[1]The "sociocentrism" which Caro Baroja speaks of as an aspect of Spanish communities (1957) would be an example of corporateness of indentity. "Corporateness" thus includes a good deal more of culture than the common, mainly jural, concept of "corporate."

[2]In Latin contexts this is most often but not always seen in ritualized competition between religious brotherhoods or between *barrio* divisions within a segmented community or, in the case of unsegmented communities, between whole communities.

[3]The vast majority of miners at these camps are long or short term transients in the término, and do not enter this study to any great extent.

[4]For complete census figures see Appendix 1.

[5]Some towns of the region appear to have reached the point of Durkheimean Anomie. Certainly the depopulation which is sweeping rural Spain has something to do with this depressed state. Almonaster, though it too is suffering out-migration, has managed to maintain some demographic equilibrium.

[6]The interested reader may consult Aguilera (1972) for a much more complete ethnographic account or wait for his second book on Almonaster.

Rites And Rituals

In any culture, ritual may be divided into two types, each with its own characteristic functional emphasis. The first is a set of rites meant to mark the transition of the individual from one state to another. This cycle of "rites of passage" is passed through by each individual during his or her lifetime.

The second type of ritual, often called "rites of intensification," is not directed at individuals nor at the permanent change in state of individuals or groups. Instead, the major functional "purpose" is the reaffirmation of desired states of whole social organizational groups. The timing of this cycle of rites is often calendrical and, as in the case of Almonaster, often strictly annual.

Although the labels used here will be Rituals of the Life Cycle and Rituals of the Annual Cycle, the actual diagnostic criteria will be functional "purpose," rather than timing. Life cycle will include only rites of passage, regardless of whether they have a fixed annual date or not. Those rites which are classified as Annual will be the rites of intensification.

The rituals of the annual cycle form the rites, or yearly "festivals," held in each community. Because of the length and public nature of these rituals they are the most apparent to the casual observer, while the ceremonies of the life cycle are often less dramatic. Nevertheless, the latter are of equal importance for the social organization of community and multicommunity. They outline the basic beliefs and understandings which are the components of the group's cultural content, and they mark the order and process by which each individual is formally invested in the cultural and social system.

15

CHAPTER 2

Rituals Of The Life Cycle: Transitions And Values

With the exception of death, each rite of passage in the life cycle represents a transition for the individual which marks the beginning of a new way of behaving. At each step the individual is expected to conform to new values, to behave in a new way. The ceremonies themselves serve not only as transition points for the individual, but also formally announce to society that it must judge the individual by a new set of standards. In this sense they mark the various developmental levels in the conscious, normative system of Almonaster culture.

The life cycle is the scheme by which the people apply the most basic of all role generating principles—sex and age. As such it supplies the basis for the social structural inventory, the basic cast of characters in the social organization of community and of multicommunity. Each person, no matter what other ascribed or achieved roles he or she may hold, is first characterized by his or her position within the life cycle. Adhesion to the rites of the life cycle, with all of their associated values and patterns, creates a substantial part of the shared experiences and expectations, and the basically similar cultural background of all of the people within the termino. Although it is quite difficult to determine the full geo-

16

graphic range of this life cycle as so many of its rites are common to large areas of Spain which implies a cultural similarity beyond the local region, it does not imply the existence of extended social boundaries. The most obvious and important reason for this is the fact that none of the life cycle rites can be used to create groups. In most cases, passage of a specific step simply means a new addition to a social category. A few of the rites, which involve the simultaneous passage by a group of initiates, are able to create horizontal networks of lasting importance in the social organization of community, but they do not create true groups in the sense of shared actions, collective responsibilities or property. Thus the values and patterns of behavior associated with the life cycle are attributes of groups, not creators of them.

BAPTISM

Although baptism is the beginning of an individual's passage through the life cycle, it marks a time in which the individual is simply a passive actor. In the baptismal rite most of the important values and new patterns of behavior are applied to close adult relatives rather than to the new baby.

Having a baby in Almonaster is seen as a fairly simple procedure. The mother has been seen by the doctor at least twice before the time of delivery, and the physician will try to be there during the last few hours. In attendance in the woman's tightly shuttered bedroom are also one or two older women who have some experience in childbirth. These women are not official midwives, but their knowledge is often quite extensive. The people of Almonaster convey the overall impression that births are easy, but painful, and that if there should be complications, which they know could prove fatal, they have consummate faith in the doctor to save the mother. The doctor comes and goes late into the night caring for the residents of the town and his patients in the aldeas.

After the birth the doctor examines both the child and the mother and the worry is over. By the third day the mother is up and doing most of her normal household chores, though she probably will not do heavy work for at least a week nor go far from the house. If the baby should be born in poor health or if it should develop any signs of weakness, then the parents will quickly line up a set of godparents and have the child immediately baptised. This precaution is taken only when the baby's death seems imminent, so that it may be buried within the consecrated walls of the cemetery.

Most babies are healthy, and the baptism preparations are more leisurely. While the mother is regaining her strength, and small, gnome-like women or "grandmothers" swathed in black who draw upon a life-time of experience colored and interpreted by "costumbre" are wondering aloud why the dropping of the abdomen and the onset of labor didn't correspond to the phases of the moon as they should have, the husband is busy. As head of the family, the father is responsible for having the name of the new baby inscribed on his family identification papers by the func-tionaries in the Ayuntamiento. At the same time, he will go to the church and arrange for the priest to baptize the child. The baptism may take place in the town church, in one of the aldea chapels, or even in one of the isolated chapels in the countryside. The date itself is set for the con-venience of the participants, but it usually takes place from fourteen to twenty-one days after the child's birth.

The parents are not, however, participants in the baptism, which is a ceremony for the child and its godparents. Since the parents commonly know ahead of time that they will need godparents, it is usually a mere formality for the father to announce the birth and ask officially that the chosen candidates become co-parents with him and his wife. The godpar-ents, a priest, and the baby itself are the only indispensable members of a baptismal ceremony.

The baptism itself, as well as the secular party following it, may be more or less elaborate. The priest is sometimes joined by several altar boys and the subchanter, all of whom are dressed in the appropriate robes. The reception may vary from a glass of sherry or brandy and a *tapa*, an hors d'oeuvre of salami, to a sumptious buffet lunch of countless kinds of *tapas* with beer, sherry, and bottled soft drinks.

Baptism and the reception are really two different ceremonies celebrat-ing two distinct transitions. The baptism represents entrance of the child into the Catholic church; the first step towards entrance into Almonaster culture and society. Consequently it is a very important step for a people whose world view includes a nebulous "null set" of non-catholics, the *Protestantes*. Associated with a kind of heretical blasphemy, *Protestan-te*, is an all inclusive category for anyone who disputes or breaks any of the basic tenets of the Roman Catholic Church in Spain. Grouped to-gether in this category are the British and French engineers and mine owners, who until recently were a "colonial" presence in the southern part of the término, local suicides, homicides and unbaptised babies. These people constitute a wide assortment of persons, some of whom are actively disliked and some of whom are pitied, but none of whom are con-sidered active upright members of the social system of Almonaster.

Although baptism is an obvious necessity for everyone in the community, it is rarely a ceremony which is elaborated.

The secular reception, in contrast, is often an elaborate ritual, into which more than one donor puts a fair amount of money. The cured meat products and bottled beverages which make up the fare are among the more expensive items of food. This reception celebrates the fruition of the marriage. Children are a happy and desired product of marriage; thus their births bring joy and happiness to their parents. Barren marriages are greatly pitied.

The reception can also be considered as a celebration of the continuation of two lines of descent, a third generation in the geneology. Thus grandparents are likely to contribute to or be totally responsible for the reception of their first grandchild. A new link of godparentship has also been formed; thus the new godfather is sometimes a contributor to the party. As a general rule, however, the elaboration of the reception tends to be in the hands of some coalition of parents and grandparents. The first such reception is almost always the grandest, with subsequent births meriting much smaller celebrations.

COMMUNION AND NIÑEZ

First Communion is the transition which marks the end of *niñez*, "childhood," and the beginning of "youth." The beginnings of social networks established through extra-familial relations are important during niñez, but the actual passage of the First Communion is just as significant because of the resulting changed values and expectations for the child.

Niñez is a time of close and almost continuous physical contact. Mother and father, siblings and countless neighbors are constantly fondling the new infant. The situation does not change appreciably when the baby has learned to toddle, except that even small children can hug and kiss the youngster when he or she is out of the cradle and onto their level. In good weather most of the streets in the town resound to the piercing screams of delight of one-year-olds and aged women alike. This is not a sham display on the part of the old women, because everyone is both captivated by and devoted to small children. As each child improves in coordination and control, the capacity for idle mischief increases, so that by the time a child reaches the age of three or four, some of the street noises include equally piercing expostulations from parents for these youngsters to behave, and the sudden tears and yells which accompany slaps and shakings. Physical contact does not decrease with age, but it is no longer all hugs and caresses. Parents and older relatives in general tend to be warm but consistently strict, perhaps even authoritarian.

By the age of five children, regardless of sex, are spending a good deal of the day in the street in front of the family house playing with others of roughly their own age. These friendships do not always last as active relationships into adult life, in part because of the tremendous wealth differences which may exist between families which live side by side. At the same time, children from both the richest and the most humble families in Almonaster may form friendships which are never totally lost. At their weakest, these friendships can be seen in the form of polite, even warm, but formal recognition during adult life. On occasion they remain as strong relationships between rich and poor. In either case, this bond formed in childhood greatly inhibits the social divergence which wealth extremes might be expected to engender.

Any failure to acknowledge these extra-familial relationships publicly would indicate the existence of some grievance between the two individuals which had resulted in a permanent falling out. Such displays are considered bad form, in-group hostility being one of the forces which an individual should have under control at all times.

Another reason for a slight cooling of these relationships within a few short years is the onset of formal schooling. In both the girls' and the boys' schools, the child sits on a bench with age-mates from the entire community. Thus each child is able for the first time to make friends on the basis of personality rather than on proximity; consequently some childhood alliances are bound to shift. Still, when the entire population of same-sex six-year-olds numbers about half a dozen, each child has a hard time not being intimate with all of them. For the boys, the communion ritual, which they will all go through at about eight years of age, is the first of two rites of passage that serves to formally set and institutionalize this local network of age-mates.

Although boys and girls interact very freely in all parts of Almonaster, which is seemingly a contradiction of the stereotyped Spanish emphasis on segregation of the sexes, First Communion is the point at which they begin to diverge. Thus First Communion is the last life cycle rite in which both boys and girls actively interact until their life cycles again cross at marriage. Certainly by their first year in school male and female roles are sharply defined, with girls already taking a more active part in women's work while the boys are still devoted to playing with their friends.

First Communion

The actual ceremony of First Communion takes place as part of the mass on Corpus Cristi.[1] The first Thursday after Trinity Sunday, it usually falls during the first part of June. Preparations for First Communion and the first confession are extensive. In the town of Almonaster, the entire spring is spent in weekly joint catechism classes held during school hours by the teachers from both schools. All children between eight and eleven or twelve who have not taken First Communion are included in these classes, but it is the parents who make the final decision about when their child will first take communion. In the case of large poor families there is often a retarding of the age of communion so that only one child will participate each year. In this way a part of the cost of First Communion is cut because each successive child can wear the same clothing with only minor alterations from year to year. For truly poverty-stricken families, the financing of the child's basic needs for participation depends upon the generosity of either wealthier community members or of the Ayuntamiento itself.

Like almost all other ceremonies in Almonaster, there is a secular finish to a religious beginning. Thus, there are two halves to the rite, which begins with a formal ritual closely linked to the basic institutions of the community, followed by a more informal, individually oriented, ritual. The First Communion Mass is followed by smaller or larger receptions in the homes of the communicants. A basic attribute of all secular rituals is the happy sharing of food, and the term used to describe this commensal gathering varies depending on the location and style of the meal. In the case of First Communion and Baptism this ritual is usually called a *refresco,* literally "refreshment." If the refreshments include elaborate, cooked dishes it may be termed a "lunch" or "dinner." The location in these cases is always within the town limits and indoors. (In other kinds of Almuñense rituals, the secular meal may be called a "picnic" because refreshments are served outside the physical boundary of the town and out of doors, or it may be another kind of indoor, in town, meal which is identified by the style or nature of the main dish. Thus some ritual meals are called "salads," "stews," and the like.)

In the town of Almonaster the Corpus Cristi mass takes place at about eleven in the morning. Everybody is in their best clothes. The men are in suits, the Guardia Civil and the two Ayuntamiento officers in dress uniforms, and the women in their finest. The children who are to take communion for the first time during the mass are dressed in white. The boys are in army or navy uniforms (officers, as well as less expensive enlisted men's uniforms) and the girls are in "bridal" dresses or nuns' habits. The presence of this relatively new ritual accoutrement has consequently made First Communion something of a burden for poorer families. The First Communicants sit on both sides of the central aisle between the normal seating area and the altar, facing the central aisle. Behind them sit their parents, also out of their regular seats. With this group sit six "important" men of Almonaster, usually members of the town council. The rest of the congregation sits in their normal seats. School children are in the first rows with the school mistress and several older girls near-by to keep them under control and to help them sing during the mass. Be-hind the children on both sides of the central aisle sit all of the women and the younger children. Finally the men and older boys all sit together in the last third of the church, separated from the women and children by a transverse aisle leading to the side door.

The bells peal, and the people start to come to church. The weather is beautiful as June is one of the perfect months in the Sierra. There is a leisurely festive air. People greet each other as they come up the streets and the steps of the church. The women and small children go directly in-to the church stopping only to cross themselves. Some of the more "devout" men also hurry in, but most men and older boys, usually the first to arrive at the church, linger outside the door talking and smoking, entering as a group just at the last moment. During a "normal" mass the priest and two altar boys are the only officiators at the altar. In the choir loft singing, responding, and playing the melodeon, is the subchanter. As one of the major masses of Almonaster, Corpus Cristi often finds more than one priest in attendance. These priests are sons of the town who have picked this time to sing mass in their home community. Also in the loft with the subchanter for this special mass, are the oldest girls who act as a church choir.

With these added personnel in attendance, this very special mass be-gins. It follows the standard liturgy, with two exceptions: communion is given twice and there is a procession by the entire congregation. The first of the two communions is for the new communicants and their parents. After they have received the Eucharist, the entire congregation leaves the church for the procession. First go three altar boys, one carrying a large staff with a silver crucifix, flanked by the other two who carry long silver candle holders. These three are representative of the entire parade structure. The two candle holders lead two equal lines of parishioners. Between these two lines go the ritual subjects and practioners as well as all of the important ritual tokens. With only one exception, every single individual has a place in this procession fixed by his or her position within the life cycle. The single exception is the subchanter who oversees the entire procession by setting the pace, keeping people in position and assuring that the proper route through town is taken. The two "secular" lines of parishioners led by the candle holders walk on the sides of the street, while the ritually charged participants walk down the center. Those parishioners who follow the candle holders take up positions similar to their seating arrangement in the church. First in these two lines come the young children who have not yet taken communion; next come the older girls who are followed by the oldest unmarried girls, married women, and smallest children. Following the women and smallest children come the younger postcommunion boys. Finally come the oldest unmarried boys and men. This is the standard parade order for all church sponsored processions. (If the parade is one in which there are heavy images to be carried, the oldest unmarried boys and younger married men are not in the "secular" lines; instead they are in the center of the street following the images which they take turns carrying.)

In the First Communion procession, the first communicants who follow the crucifer and his silver cross, make up the initial component of the ritually charged personnel. Walking two and three abreast, each first communicant carries a prayer book and rosary and some of the girls carry baskets of flower petals. This group, the main body of communicants, walks between that segment of the secular lines which includes mothers and small children, a considerable distance behind the silver cross which leads the entire procession. Following the communicants, again at a distance, comes a group whose center is the Host in a special silver and glass case carried by the priest. This Host-centered group marches between the ends of the two lines at the level of the oldest unmarried boys and men. This final ritual group is led by an altar boy who carries the incensor. Two of the first communicant boys who act as altar boys and carry glass enclosed candles follow the incensor. Behind these three boys march the six respected/important men. These men support the six poles of a canopy which shades the priest and Host. Last come all of the secondary priests in attendance. (Some of the church sponsored processions merit an armed guard of honor. In this case the Host has a guard of two Guardia Civiles in dress uniform who carry machine guns. These two flank the canopy.)

The procession follows the standard church procession route, which leads out of the church plaza to the central plaza, where it passes the private chapel but not the ayuntamiento. From the central plaza it goes down the hill toward the west and the plaza of the Cross of the Fountain, then it heads back to the central plaza and on toward the eastern side of town and the plaza of the Cross of the Llano. Finally it returns to the church. As in all church processions, the object is to include the two monumental crosses at each side of town in the ritual. The entire town is covered symbolically by the procession. During this procession a short stop is also made in the doorway of the chapel where a short prayer and blessing is offered by the priests while the procession continues without them. This is one of the few instances where the subchanter as overseer of the procession is really needed. He must slow the procession sufficiently for the priests to return to their positions without having to use undignified haste.

The two monumental crosses and the plazas in which they are located have been decorated for the occasion of this procession by their respective brotherhoods. Waiting in each plaza is a small group of spectators, mostly old men and women and mothers with young children. Within the plaza is a wide aisle of marsh grass or eucalyptus leaves, lined with potted plants. As the procession reaches the plaza the two secular lines walk on the outside of this green carpet which leads directly to the cross. As they reach the cross, the secular participants form a rough circle of spectators. The ritually charged part of the procession then walks on the leafy path. First come the communicants, with the girls sprinkling flower petals from their baskets. They stop a little way from the cross and are soon passed by the Host group, which proceeds to the foot of the cross where the priest brings the Host out from under the canopy for the blessing ceremony. At both crosses the ritual is repeated. Each cross is decorated with a profusion of cut and potted flowers. A decorated cloth covers the stone base of each cross and a silk scarf is draped over each of the crosses. A painted or sculpted representation of Christ on the cross covers the front of each stone base.

Once back in the church, the mass is completed with a second communion for the congregation, and the religious part of the ritual is ended. While each first communicant's family holds a reception, the communicants themselves go around the neighborhood giving out printed cards with a religious scene on one side and the communicant's name and the date on the back. In exchange for this souvenir of the first communion, one customarily gives the child a small gift of money. Meanwhile, at the reception in the child's honor, the parents entertain neighbors, relatives and important people. The reception may include both a refresco and a "lunch." One major difference between the nature of festivities at varying economic levels is the use to which invitations to receptions are put. Poorer families use these invitations to reaffirm ties between themselves and the important people of the town. Thus some rather important, rich, or influential people can be seen entering the humblest of houses to accept an invitation to the refresco of one of the communicants. In the richer families, these "important people" are either parents, relatives or friends who may or may not be invited, and whose presence or absence is indicative of very little. After the refresco, it is quite common for a close friend of the family or relatives to remain for a fancy lunch.

First communion is considered by most people to be one of the most important and most memorable rites of a person's youth, representing the end of childish ignorance and the beginning of adult responsibility in the eyes of the church. Before first communion, the child is not allowed to receive confession and absolution, but his or her sins are considered to be sins of ignorance. Now that child is supposed to be aware and accountable for his or her acts. This is the church's point of view, but it does not differ markedly from the expections of the people of Almonaster. Each small gift which the child receives is invariably accompanied by the admonition:"Now that you have taken first communion we all expect that you will be more serious and behave better; you're not a baby anymore; now you have to behave." At the same time first communion is a joyful occasion. The child is at last a full-fledged member of the community, though not a mature member. Now the emphasis is on the process of maturation, not on gaining entrance to the society. A standard criticism of the First Communion sermon given by the priest each year is that he dwells too much on the new and heavy responsibilities, that he uses the occasion to chastise the adults for not being "religious" enough when he should be addressing himself to the joyful achievement of the children on "their day."

There are two quite distinct functions of this rite of passage. As a ceremony of initiation, it marks a new state for the initiate with new expectations of him or her on the part of the community as a whole. Actual behavior will be a long time in changing, but the basic transition that has been made is the key to the on-going process of social maturation; the child is now responsible to the community as a group where before he was responsible to his family. From the point of view of the church this is a process which takes place overnight, the act of will. For the community it is only a beginning, the desired result will only come after further training. Although there is new emphasis on self-conscious decision making, taking into account the effects of each action, and increased emphasis on self-control, no one expects a sudden change. Although these youngsters are now full community members, they are also children who will make many mistakes. Thus the community does not expect to see a dramatic change until the next life cycle rite.

The second function of the first communion ritual involves the parents
and certain informal Patron/Client-like relations. Here it is the reception
that is important, not the religious ritual. The invitation extended by the
"client" parents to the "patron" guest is a way of reciprocating for the
help given through the years by the "patron." The patronage involved is
of an informal type, but the relationship is asymmetrical enough so that
the "client" could never hope to "pay it back." At this festivity certain
individuals emerge as "patrons." Foremost among these are the drug-
gist, who gives gifts to the poorer children at Christmas time, and the
medical doctor, whose good will and kindly concern is particularly apparent during the childhood years. Standard patrons, rich farmers and
businessmen, are included to a lesser extent. The "patrons" most
honored at this time are those who stand in an informal godfather position to the child by virtue of their actions. Actual godparents are normally invited, but as "family" and not as "honored guest."

LA QUINTA AND JUVENTUD

La Quinta, "the draft," is the "official" reason for the next rite of passage which boys go through. Spanish law demands that every able-bodied
male be inducted into military service. This element of the "great tradition" in local community culture is the occasion of an exceedingly important transition in the lives of the boys. On the third Sunday in February
when each year's draftees come to the ayuntamiento for their group
physical, they pass from *juventud*, "youth," to full social adulthood.[2]
This is the Day of the *Quinto*.

Each yearly levy of recruits is known as the *quinto* of a particular year;
for example, "the Quinto of '68." Individual members of such an age
grade call age mates *quinto* as a term of address and speak of "my
quinto" or "his quinto" as a term of reference. Theoretically, each boy is
in this relationship with every Spanish draftee of his own year. In the
community and multicommunity context, this function of the rite of
passage has initial importance at the community level, less initial importance at the multicommunity level, and no importance at a wider extension until the recruit actually gets to military camp.

On the Day of the Quinto all of the quintos are in their twenty-first
calendar year, although most of the boys will celebrate their actual birth-
day in the following months. Ten to thirteen years have passed since
these boys took their First Communion, and a considerable number of
significant things have happened to them. For most of the quintos,

school was over at about fourteen years of age when they had completed seven grades. A select one or two, who because of wealth or exceptional ability have gone to secondary school in other parts of the state, are also present. The majority, the stay-at-homes, go through a year or two when they are at rather loose ends. Fourteen is too young for all but a very few wage earning positions, and at home many have only part-time work to do, such as helping their fathers in the gardens. In the aldeas where a more fully agrarian pattern is followed, these boys often become full-time workers in the family farm. In general, the boys of Almonaster, rich or poor, are unable to do adult wage labor and are not in full-scale farming families which can find work to keep them busy. Poor boys do certain kinds of women's harvesting labor, and richer boys do nothing at all. By sixteen some boys have become apprentices; others have become agricultural laborers for their fathers or the land owners. Still many are jobless; the pattern of minifundia means a land shortage which is first felt by teenage boys who are superfluous to much of the family's agricultural cycle. Boys of this age do not enter into renting agreements with land owners nor do their fathers act for them since they will be leaving for military service in a few years. During the former period when the traditional latifundia agricultural system was at its peak, this group of relatively unskilled youths tended to be employed, or at least kept productively busy, by their families.

Today there is an alternative which was not as available in the past. Boys of sixteen in Almonaster can go to other parts of Spain, usually the large urban centers, and look for jobs as stock boys or clerks. Such boys always stay with relatives in the cities, and the availability of lodgings with a relative becomes one of the criteria for deciding whether a boy can leave town and go to the city. This exodus is short-lived because the jobs that these boys get are almost always bad ones. Employers are unwilling to invest much in them since they will not only be of draft age soon, but will also have to go home before that to take the induction physical.

This pre-Quinto period is a transitional one in more than economic roles. Not yet an adult, drinking and smoking are not "allowed." Boys often smoke and sometimes drink but always out of sight of their parents or any of their parents' friends. In such small communities this means that they can't do any of these things in front of adults. Thus two key adult social patterns, drinking and smoking in the bars and public places, are closed to them.

Male-female relations are also in a transitional state during this period of "youth." The boys and girls are not segregated and social interaction is free, easy and rewarding. Sexual intercourse among this local group is almost non-existent. Boys and girls mix freely in the public places of the

town; that is, on the streets and plazas. No chaperons are needed since
these public places are never empty. When sexual encounters do occur, as
happens from time to time, they are almost always conducted with outsiders. At this age a young person would be "stupid" to have relations
with a member of his or her own *pandilla* or "gang." The ideal is a brief
encounter, not a long relationship. The boys go to festivals and dances in
the other small towns and hope; the girls dance with out-of-towners at
the local dances and festivals and dream.

Frustration and sexual fantasy seem to characterize the boys and girls
from fourteen to nineteen. Boys who are actually able to achieve a few
"conquests" are revered by their peers. In the past, sexual intercourse at
this age was more common for two reasons. First, most boys had their
initial sexual encounters with prostitutes in the large towns in other
términos. Cortegana, only seven kilometers away, was a favorite spot.
Almonaster itself was "too small' to have its own prostitute. Now
prostitution is illegal in Spain, and boys of today, lacking proper training, tend to be shy and not overly confident. Only an occasional rake appears, and then he is usually the close friend of an older man who himself
was a libertine in his day. In Almonaster a boy must have training in
order to be a rake for such behavior runs counter to the values which he is
supposed to be learning at this time.

A second reason for the decrease in sexual contacts has been the general decline in population. Fewer people has meant that the young people's
groups have tended to have a wider age spread than in the past when age
mates often formed separate groups. The presence of eleven and twelve-
year-olds has tended to inhibit activities of the eighteen-year-olds even
during times of "sexual license."

Commensurate with the immature status of young people at this age,
especially for boys, true marriage is not considered a possibility under
any circumstances. Should a girl or woman become pregnant by a boy of
pre-quinto status, he rarely, if ever, is forced to marry her. Rather, she
will have the child. Later she may or may not marry depending more on
her personality than on anything else. There is no stigma attached to il-
legitimacy for the child, and normally none for the mother. Although
there is no stigma for the mother in a moral sense, she is considered to be
"stupid," since it is the woman's responsibility to guard against con-
ception by forcing her partner to practice coitus interruptus because "of
his own accord, no man is likely to be careful." Except for being considered a rake, no stigma is attached to the father, as he was only
"naturally" taking advantage of the situation. On very rare occasions
two young people may marry because of a pregnancy, but this is normal-

ly due to the importance of the relationship between the parents. The newlyweds don't live together under such conditions, and the boy is not responsible economically until he is in the military when he is expected to send his pay to his wife. At this point his parents may take her in. Since he is already married, the boy is unable to fully participate in the normal activities of his age mates, and he does not enjoy the adult status or privileges of a married man. Such marriages are quite rare.

The advent of sexuality at this age illustrates an apparent contradiction in the value system of Almonaster. A basic belief of the Almuñenses is that human beings will take advantage, *aprovecharse*, of their surroundings in order to maximize their situation, and within limits this is a positive virtue. Boys are *not* taught to "take advantage of girls," per se, but in other areas of life this is certainly a consciously inculcated virtue. Perhaps most apparent in terms of economics and resources, this general virtue is supposed to be evident in the way a boy applies himself to any task or job he is given. Although he is not trained to take advantage of women, a boy in Almonaster is trained to take advantage of other "things."

In most areas of interpersonal relations, taking advantage of the situation to the point of hurting someone else is considered extremely improper. The exercise of self-awareness and self-control is a most basic value. Yet the sexual situation appears at first glance to be an exception to this. Here the value of control is opposed by the strongly held belief in the inability of men to control themselves. It is widely held that in the area of sex, no man can control his basic desire to maximize his situation. Thus the statement "A man is like a donkey, put him in a room alone with a woman, any woman except perhaps his mother, and he will *try* to screw her" is common among the men of the town. Under such circumstances, it is supposedly the woman's responsibility to protect *both* of their honors. In practice most men who feel that this is the "natural state of man," or "of the Andalucian," go to great pains not to be put into a situation of conflict where they will feel compelled to uphold their image as a man by contradicting the basic value of self-control and proper behavior. A woman rarely has to work at rebuffing the advances of a man under these circumstances. In fact women are unaware that they have been in the presence of a "sex-crazed" male, since a man can usually "tell" when a woman will be unreceptive to his advances. Not wishing to make a scene for the whole town to talk about, he then alters his behavior since it wouldn't be successful anyhow. "It is after all a fact that a woman can't be made to have intercourse against her will except by knocking her out." In the folklore of sexuality, the woman has the responsibili-

ty for self-control, for following the rules, for being aware of the social
consequences. In practice, however, the man behaves as though he were
as responsible here as he is in all other areas of life.

Day of the Quinto

The basic value of self-control, social responsibility, and careful following of the rules is called *formalidad*, and one is or is not *formal*. To be
adult, is to be *formal*. Except for the area of sex, this is a value which applies equally to men and to women.[4] This value, and the adult status that
it is synonymous with, are the central themes of the Quinto ritual. As is
often the case in Almonaster, the central value being honored is reified by
behaving in exactly the opposite manner during the ritual itself. While a
person's formalidad should be evident in everything he or she does, for
men there is an especially critical area. This critical area involves the
heavy social drinking which men engage in during the evenings. In the
etiquette of social drinking, there is great emphasis on always being in
control; one does not drink to the point of losing self-control. Beyond this
point the individual becomes a burden on others, makes a fool of himself,
or worst of all, insults people and makes a general commotion. Thus a
formal person does not drink to the point of staggering, falling down, or
general clumsiness, nor does he allow the alcohol to loosen his tongue. A
formal person is never lewd in mixed company. Since social drinking involves a number of shot-sized drinks per night, a man may quite easily
become rather drunk without realizing it. Since dirty jokes are also a
major amusement for men, the prohibition on lewd talk becomes more
meaningful. Thus it is hardly surprising that the Quinto ritual honoring a
boy's entrance into adulthood is characterized by extreme drunkenness
and loud, lewd, public singing and joking.

Like the other life cycle ceremonies, the Day of the Quinto has a public
ritual followed by a more private one. The second ritual is, as usual,
characterized by a special meal.

On the morning of the Sunday that is to be the Day of the Quinto, all of
the boys who will be this year's Quinto assemble, with moral support
from older brothers and friends, in their respective communities. Each
group starts with a number of drinks. In a short time the group is ready
to make the rounds of the community singing a series of dirty songs. The
women are expected to stay indoors. Pressed close to shuttered doors and
windows, laughing at the verses, they thoroughly enjoy themselves.
This is only the beginning. After more drinks at the local bar, the entire

group sets out for the town of Almonaster, which itself has been regaled by the local Quinto. As each aldea group reaches the outskirts of town, they make a grand entrance. Singing their songs, they stagger arm-in-arm up the center of the street, stopping at all the bars along their way to the central square where the ayuntamiento stands. As each new contingent arrives it is informally identified and soon all the spectators know the aldea affiliation of every group. As all the groups congregate at the bar on the corner of the central plaza, many of the youths are at the point of falling down. As a boy reaches that ghastly shade of dead white which preceeds passing out, his companions drape him over one of the benches in the plaza to dry out a bit. Soon he is back in the fray.

With their songs and drinking, the boys are a good show for the spectators who comment on many things; never failing to point out how each community's youth perpetuates its hometown characteristics. One group is "obviously more brutish because they come from such and such aldea"; another group is "just as shifty as their fathers before them"; or "the people from that aldea were always stupid. Look, see how they act." This is an especially good time for such community stereotyping since, in their extreme drunkenness, one can impute any number of characteristics to the boys' behavior.

Before too many have passed out, at about noon, the senior doctor arrives at the ayuntamiento and the first group staggers into the building and up the steps to the second floor council room where they are given their military physical. There is still more horseplay and merriment as they descend into the street. The favorite joke is writing a person's height or weight on his back with chalk, and insinuating the number on his back corresponds to the length of his penis. The official public ceremony is now over and each group staggers back to its home. Once reassembled at the home of one of their members, or some suitable meeting place, they begin the second part of the ritual.

The second part of the ritual is called a *guiso* or "stew" because the traditional main course is just that, a goat stew. The meal begins with *tapas* of cured salami and other pork products, plenty of bread, and white wine. Then the main course arrives, a great bowl of stew. Traditionally each person gets a tablespoon and stands around the small table with the common stew bowl. Each person has a glass or cup and bread. The main course begins. In the small aldea homes, the room is packed. The quintos often have to stand sideways to the table in order for all of them to eat at once. Behind them stand fathers and other relatives helping to keep their glasses full and handing in more bread and new bowls of stew. All the while the merriment is at a high pitch. A favorite game is *bola* or *dar bola*.

One person sticks his spoon in the stew and leaves it standing there, at the same times he says, "bola"—"hold it!" Everyone is supposed to stop eating until either the spoons falls down (which with a good goat stew may never happen) or someone dips his spoon and without permission takes more stew. The person who thus breaks the *"bola"* is penalized by having to drink a full glass of wine all at once, or having to drink a full shoe of wine, or some such equally enjoyable stunt. Because of the noise and the crowding, there is always someone who didn't hear the "bola" announced and a great deal of good natured discussion takes place before someone finally accepts the penalty. When it seems that everyone is about to burst, the entire party goes outside where there is room to breathe.

The main course is by now decorating everyone's good clothes and the floor of the room is awash. Outside there is another small table and a new set of tablespoons and even more spectators. Sisters and mothers and grandmothers and small children form a happy gallery as the wine glasses are filled again and dessert is served. There are great bowls of rice pudding to be eaten communally with the same rules as the stew, and more hilarious rounds of bola, and more drinking. By midafternoon only a very few stalwarts are left. They compete to see who can drink the most or who can drink out of the worst container; old shoes and broken flower pots are common, and wise mothers have hidden the chamber pot on this occasion. Soon all of the quintos have been overtaken by sleep and the Quinto ritual is over.

The transformation expected by the community is an important one. The boys are now allowed to drink and smoke publicly and to participate and compete in the adult status hierarchy. Formalidad is taken for granted by everyone. A public breach of formalidad will call forth lectures and "advice" form all other adults. The function of the Quinto ritual as the final initiation into the mysteries of adulthood is clear. A man is now able to marry, to be a godfather, to participate in all adult activities and is held responsible, as an adult, for all of his actions. This is the most important of all adult ceremonies for a man; marriage, fatherhood and death are secondary. There are in every generation men who will not pass through all of these secondary adult experiences; nevertheless they are considered full adult participants in the community.

A clear indication of the initiation function of this externally imposed draft can be seen in the participation of physically handicapped boys. Since the draft physical is administered by the senior doctor of the término and the local draft paperwork is done by him and the secretary of the Ayuntamiento, it is not necessary for the physically handicapped to appear at the physical. Such a boy's condition is common knowledge to the secretary, and he has been in the doctor's care all along. His records are simply forwarded as proof of his inability to serve. Legally, the handicapped boy need not attend. Social reality is otherwise.

Among the six boys from Almonaster who were the Quinto of '69 was one such handicapped boy. Francisco Pozas Valencia, officially recorded in the census as "paralytic," had suffered from muscular dystrophy, a progressive, usually fatal, neuromuscular disease, since the age of eight or nine years. Paco's inclination coincided with the doctor's advice: to live as normal a life as was possible. Confined to a wheel chair, Paco was always present at youth activities, and always included by his friends. He excelled at singing, composing and playing the harmonica. In spite of his handicap, he was happily active in the life of the town. By the time he was ready to undergo the Quinto ritual, his disease was well-advanced. Yet it never occurred either to him or to his age-mates that he not go through the ritual. Although they knew that physically his participation was not a good idea, neither his parents nor the doctor felt that they should even try to dissuade him. In the end, he participated fully in every phase of the ritual. Not to have done so would not have been a capitulation to his disease; instead it would have been a sentence to eternal social immaturity.

One of the reasons that Paco was able to go through the entire ritual was the help he received from his age-mates during the ritual itself. This help not only illustrates some of the rights and duties which can be invoked in the name of friendship, but also symbolizes the special relationship which pertains between a person and his quintos. This is a second function of the Quinto ritual. The creation of a lifelong age-set, whose shared membership is more important than the possible social disparity which characterizes its individual members. This age-set cuts across all other social categories and memberships. Rich and poor alike are in a special relationship, a special identity which can be invoked by the use of the *quinto* term of address, because the term reminds an age-mate of their special mutual relationship. Young men who were less than close friends before the ritual will now commonly use the *quinto* term to invoke this bond following the ceremony.

Boys from different communities use the common membership in the same Quinto to create ties with the local group in which they may find themselves. At a dance or festival, in the absence of previous close friendship or kinship ties, vague acquaintances may be reinforced by the quinto relationship. In their first real contact with the rest of Spain, the new recruits take this age-set membership with them to camp where they can apply it to all of the other recruits they meet there. A symbol of identity and membership exists prior to the formation of the actual camp group. In the years after active service, this quinto relationship remains a primary reference point.

Within the community itself, the quinto relationship gradually becomes overlain by countless other ties so that it becomes a bit of common community knowledge rather than an active relationship. In these later years its remaining function is to serve as a strong tie between communities which people may invoke in order to underline or to increase many other, often economic, relationships. For the old-timers, the *quinto* relationship serves as an indispensable storytelling device. In the absence of any primary kinship links, a man may be readily identified simply by establishing his quinto relationship with some other known individual.

MARRIAGE AND JUVENTUD

Marriage is the end product of the *noviazgo* relationship, the rough equivalent to "going steady" and being "engaged." As a life cycle ritual, it is more important for the woman than for the man. Without marriage a woman remains socially immature, relegated to the status and behavior of nineteen- and twenty-year-olds, until the age of forty when she is finally classed as an old maid. Once the community considers her an old maid, *soltera*, she is accepted as an adult. Nevertheless, courtesy requires that she be addressed as *señorita*, "Miss," the designation for the young unmarried-but-still-hoping girls. The majority of men in Almonaster marry, but a significant number of women become old maids; marriage which is taken for granted by men, is not a certainty for women.

Anxiety about finding a husband is not apparent in the young girls. Youth is not the transitional state for girls that it is for boys. Ambiguity of roles is not present, and time does not hang heavily for them. The years after primary school are not idle. As they grow up, girls are more involved in the adult roles of women than boys are in the adult male roles. Most girls spend a large part of the day helping in the home. They accompany their mothers to the store, an adult women's social center, where they gradually progress from being passive spectators to being more and more active links in the gossip system.

As young girls, they spend a good deal of the time playing. As they grow older, the girls spend more of their time sewing and walking with other girl friends. At the same time, boys are changing from playmates to potential *novios* in the girls' eyes. At first girls sew as practice in this necessary woman's art, but by the age of fifteen or sixteen, each girl begins her trousseau, a sewing job that will occupy a good deal of her time during the next five or six years. In addition to long afternoons of such sewing, groups of girls actively engage in dressmaking. In the evening, in fresh clothes, the girls walk out to the plaza or along the tree-lined road. In small groups, arm in arm, they laugh and talk, teasing the boys both by their comments and by their separation from them. The boys, meanwhile, alternate between showing off and ignoring the girls.

At other times boys and girls are often seen joking and playing together. Games and dancing are common not only during dances and festivals, but also at weekly "youth dances" held by the local chapter of the *Organización Juvenil de España* (O.J.E.) to which all town children belong. This is a government youth group run by older children and a few young adults. (It is a good "political" beginning for the young adult in charge.) The Frente Juvenil, as it is known, has a room in a public building where it holds dances and has tables and chairs for games and other social activities which bring boys and girls together.

Before the appearance of the O.J.E. in Almonaster, children danced *sevillanas* to their own sung and clapped accompaniment, but with a record player, they can dance modern popular dances as well as the traditional ones. Thus the change which the O.J.E. has wrought has not been in terms of increased social interaction of adolescents, but in a partial change in the dance forms.

Between the ages of about seventeen and nineteen, the girls start to consider the boys more carefully. First there is the beginning of the noviazgo relationship, which is meant to end in marriage. Initially this relationship is flexible and unofficial, equivalent to the American "going steady." Normally the couple is quite close in age, with the boy only a year or two older. Some couples last through this phase and into the next, but most couplings are short-term. There is little stigma attached to a girl at this age who has several boys. Other people ordinarily refer to the boy and girl as *novios* ("fiancé and fiancée"), but the usage here is, at least in part, a way of teasing. The couple walks and talks and dances together. Sometimes the boy or girl will try to make his or her partner jealous by walking, talking or dancing with another when the intended victim is not present.

This behavior contrasts with the conduct of true "novios." The boys never become true novios until they have at least passed the Quinto ritual (and for most not until they have returned from their military duty). Once entered into, the true novio relationship should not be broken. If it does break and the girl is at fault, she will have a hard time finding another novio and may never marry. If the boy is at fault, then the girl is not "penalized" and her reputation stays intact. But a girl who is victimized several times and repeatedly has the true novio relationship fall through is considered spoiled and will find it difficult to marry.

True novios walk and talk and dance together like their unofficial counterparts, but in addition the boy is welcome at the girl's house. He achieves this privilege by asking her father for his permission to court and marry his daughter. Until this is done and permission granted, the boy and girl's father practice a social ignorance when they are together in public. The boy pretends that he is just another townsman, and the father does the same. The boy would never be caught on the doorstep by the girl's father. When a true novio enters the military, he sends home money to his novia; she, in turn, may actually make extended visits to his parents' house.

Two related factors are important for understanding the relationship between novios and the strategy of courtship. First, there is the shortage of boys from the age of about eighteen to the late twenties. This demographic imbalance results, in part, from the boys who spend a year or two in the cities before they go through the Quinto ceremony. In addition the year to two years of active military service eliminates almost every twenty-one to twenty-three-year old. After military service, a few boys come home with wives from the outside; others come home again, but they soon leave to work in other parts of Europe for several years. Finally, there are always some boys who never really come home at all, who stay in the cities permanently.

A second factor affecting the novio relationship is the greater mobility of boys. While the girls are more or less restricted to the social events within the community and the multicommunity, the boys are free to go from one community to the next within the multicommunity and beyond. When all else fails, a boy may pedal for several hours on a bicycle to get to an event he considers important. Neither of these factors works in favor of the girls. Although most girls seem to have little trouble marrying, there is a sizable minority who are not so fortunate.

If a girl does not become novios with a community-mate, either because she will not accept any of them or they won't or can't accept her, there is no initial obstacle to her being courted by someone from any of the other communities in the area. On occasion, a girl from a small aldea will come to visit or live with someone in the town of Almonaster where there are more prospects. More often, however, a propitious meeting at a community festival or a dance leads a boy to continue to see the girl by traveling to her home. Such a suitor usually arrives in the community sometime between four and six on a weekend afternoon. He can see the girl up until dinner time. After dinner he may meet her again. If he has relatives or other close connections in the locality, he will spend the interim with them. If he has no local contacts, he will pass the time in one of the bars. In either event, he will spend some time in the bar, if only for an after dinner coffee before seeing the girl again.

This is a crucial time for both the suitor and the girl. While in the bar the suitor is being reviewed by the other men in the town. They can accept him, in which case he blends in rather easily, or they can try to discourage him in a number of subtle ways. These ways vary from simply trying to make him feel uncomfortable, to telling him lies in order to make him distrust the girl. Should the relationship persist in spite of this harrassment, poison-pen letters sometimes start arriving at his home town addressed to his parents or the local priest. These letters, like the lies, malign the girl, and their object is to have his family put pressure on him to forget her. Occasionally poison-pen letters are also used to warn a girl that her out of town suitor is being unfaithful to her or that he is already married.

In both cases it is the girl who inevitably suffers. If the town feels motivated enough to spoil her relationship, and she persists in picking suitors whom the town won't accept, she will have a string of failed novioships, and inevitably her reputation will be so sullied that it will be difficult, if not impossible, for her to marry within the context of the community. The rationale for her loss of reputation is two-fold. First, the common expectation is that at some point novios may have sexual intercourse (which is no problem if they eventually marry). Second, the more novios a girl has had, the greater the probability that she has had relations with at least one of them. Suspected of having had relations with several men, the girl is consequently considered a poor bet to become a stable wife. Unless the girl becomes pregnant, these suspicions are never based on anything more tangible than circumstantial evidence. The girl often never finds out what has happened, and the community at large never changes its treatment of her, but she is fated never to have a hometown novio. Many of the possible novios from within the multicommunity will be forewarned by their friends and relations as to her poor reputation. As she ages, suitors from without the multicommunity will increasingly be apt to try to take advantage of her. Thus a truly vicious cycle is set up which militates against the girl, one which is only broken in the rarest of instances.

That an attempt is made to maintain a kind of corporate control over community connubium rights is only a little less intriguing than the manner in which the decision to accept or reject a suitor is made. Two kinds of criteria seem to be implied: first, the nature of personal ties between the suitor and members of the community; and, second, the nature of the traditional relationship between the suitor's home community and the community of the girl. Personal ties can smooth the way, but community-level relationships dominate the decision. Certain communities frequently exchange marriage partners. These community level relationships correspond to the limits of the multicommunity. Thus control of marriage for all but the richest residents seems to be a basic function of the multicommunity.

Although the multicommunity is a relatively endogamous system, it is not a genetically closed one. A suitor from without the multicommunity may avoid the "gauntlet" of townsmen by becoming a resident of the town. Having thus become a junior member of the corporation, he is free to court whom he pleases. Historically, the multicommunity tends to grow by both fission and fusion so that marriage patterns shift with time to include new community populations. At the same time, some communities, which are no longer members of the multicommunity even though recognized kin ties abound, fade out of the marriage network.[5]

The means by which the community attempts to control connubium rights presents another basic paradox within Almuñense value structure. Closely related to the normative value of fomalidad is the concept of being *pueblerino*, a value which encourages each member of the community to be very concerned with the community's image. This pride in community image expresses itself in at least two ways: by a devotion of the individual's energies toward the development or beautification of the town; and, by a desire that every visitor leave with only the most superlative impressions of the people and the town. The hostile treatment of some of the out-of-town suitors is clearly in direct contradiction to this often expressed value. Consequently extreme secrecy surrounds the authorship of a poison-pen letter. While many people deplore the treatment of some suitors, they also feel that under extenuating circumstances this unfriendly treatment may be justified. Such loopholes in the *pueblerino* value serve therefore as a rationale for writing poison-pen letters: "It is not right to deal with anyone in this way, but this time it turned out to be necessary."

In terms of the ritual of the life cycle, the way an individual secures a mate is secondary to the fact of having found one. Because most men do not marry until their late twenties or early thirties, the official novio relationship usually continues for several years after a man returns from his military service. Once the official noviazgo is entered into, there can be no improper behavior on the part of the young woman. She should be extremely careful not to participate in any situation which might make her novio jealous. At dances which he does not attend, she may dance with her father or brother, but she is even more prudent if she dances only with girl friends. The man must also be more careful since his treatment of the noviazgo responsibility is considered an indication of his formalidad. Tacit permission is given for idle dalliance far from home, but within the multicommunity, it is considered bad form. In addition, when a man is known to be novios with someone, no proper girl would even consent to dance with him. Thus chances for even a fleeting relationship within the multicommunity are slim, as there is always someone in the local community who knows the status of a man from even the most distant aldea. Word quickly passes to one of the girl's friends or relatives who will immediately walk out into the middle of the dance floor to inform the girl that her partner has such a relationship. As soon as one girl finds out that he has a *compromiso,* an "engagement," she warns all the rest and they all cease interaction with him, lest any one of them be accused of impropriety.

Although the official noviazgo relationship changes the status and sanctioned behavior expected of the individual and of the community with respect to the individual, there is no ceremony or official announcement. Nevertheless the new behavior, rights, and duties expected of a novio are not temporary attributes. The rules of conduct associated with the noviazgo relationship are perpetuated by the marriage ceremony. In this sense, marriage itself is more of a symbolic institutionalization of noviazgo behavior than the start of new patterns. Certainly sanctioned sexual relations and a new economic unit are adjuncts of the marriage ritual, but they tend to be mechanical adjustments overshadowed by the behavioral and status changes that are begun by noviazgo.

The Wedding

Although weddings in Almonaster are often festive occasions followed by sumptuous receptions, they generally are not as significant a ritual as they might be. As in other receptions, a number of Patron/Client-like relationships may be acknowledged by invitations to attend. But two potentially significant roles, the *"padrinos* of the wedding," are largely under utilized. These "godparents" do not form formal relationships with the true parents; instead they are rather close friends and/or relations of the couple. The honor of having been the *padrinos* has, however, little ongoing impact on this friendship or on any other relationship. In addition, the relationship is not used to finance the ceremony, as the couple's parents support the bulk of that burden. On occasion, prestigious individuals are chosen as padrinos to enhance the ceremony, but this distinction does not form a lasting link between the Padrino and the family because it is usually the result of pre-existing Patron/Client or friendship relation.

The couple and their padrinos meet at the bride's house. Inside, the bride is attended by her friends and relatives as she dresses. The groom and most of the guests gather in another room or in front of the house. Brides wear modern white bridal gowns, and the groom wears a suit and white shirt. In addition, the groom wears a tie, an especially dressy touch.[6] When everything is ready and the guests have all arrived, the bride and groom are escorted from the house. The padrino escorts and bride and the madrina escorts the groom, following them come the families and guests. After a Roman Catholic mass and ceremony, the bride and groom emerge to the ringing of the church bell and the throwing of rice or grain. They lead the way to the reception where the bride and groom will sit with their parents and the priest, while all of their friends enjoy themselves at side tables.

While few couples go on a "honeymoon," everyone recognizes that it will take some time for the couple to adjust to each other. The woman's behavior in particular, is explained by the phrase, "these are the first months." Both have new duties and responsibilities. They have established a new economic unit, even if they do not immediately set up an independent household. The husband starts gardening on his own. Until now, his gardening has been in the *huerta* of his father or other close relative. As an independent gardener, he will be under the eyes of the whole community. The way in which he handles his garden will demonstrate whether he lives up to the important virtue of being a "good gardener" *(buen hortelano)*. This is a change which usually accompanies marriage, but it is not generated by marriage alone since the gardening virtue is linked only to gardening itself. Marriage is also the commonest way of gaining political suffrage.

In the eyes of Almuñenses, the most important reason for marriage is children: "They are the joy of the marriage. By their presence they create Happiness." They seem to represent continuity and well-being. In old age children are the moral as well as the physical solace of the aged couple. In terms of social organization, children are the only means to personal control of the important adult relationship of *compadrazgo*, "coparentship." Since compadrazgo ties are initiated by the parents of the new-born child, one is never able to choose his *compadres* until he has children. Without children one must wait to be chosen.

DEATH

Death brings on the last major life cycle rite which a person goes through. Unlike other rituals, the funeral starts with a family-oriented rite, the wake, and ends with a community rite, the burial. Although the actual state of being after death is debated, the importance of being buried within the walls of the *campo santo*, "sanctified cemetery," is recognized by all. Burial as a community ritual recognizes and finalizes the change in status of one of its members. Burials are attended by the majority of all adult men in the town almost without regard to the actual identity of the deceased. The family-oriented wake is the more important rite in terms of the personality and position of the deceased and his or her family. The wake thus varies in size and relative importance depending on the status and position of the person and the family. Empirically, the only status changes involve the close living relatives of the deceased.

The quality of the funeral and the permanence of the burial are the traditional concerns which relate to the material status of the deceased. In the past there were three classes of funeral. For a third class funeral, which was the cheapest, the body was not taken into the church but simply brought up to the door. The priest wore his most threadbare vestments. Great emphasis was placed on not having this class of funeral if it were at all possible. Church practices have been liberalized, and third class funerals are no longer held. Now all funerals are the same, only varying in attendance and some kinds of elaboration.

In contrast, the actual burial still comes in several classes. Most expensive is the permanent niche. The cemetery in Almonaster is bounded by a high wall and against this on the inside are tiers of niches, like boxes in a post office. These niches may be rented or bought. If rented and the rent is past due, out come the remains and the niche is ready for a new occupant. The ousted remains are unceremoniously thrown into a communal ossuary. Less expensive than the niches are burial plots in the ground within the cemetery. These, too, may be had on a permanent or rented basis. As in the past, the criterion used to decide what type of funeral and burial the deceased would receive is the amount the survivors could pay. Burial niches are still rented and sold, but the increase in cash in circulation in the last decades has seen a rise in niche purchases. Often more than one family member occupies each niche.

One of the major public contributions of the present término administration has been in the area of the material status of the dead. Since the purchase of a Plymouth hearse, every member of the término is entitled to its services. The hearse should pick up the coffin at the home of the deceased, but because most of the streets in Almonaster are not navigable to any motor traffic, it usually waits for the deceased at the church and then takes the coffin to the cemetery three-quarters of a mile away. When someone dies in the aldeas, most of which use the cemetery at Almonaster, the hearse goes to the aldea to bring the coffin to the church in Almonaster. Previously, a truck was hired or the coffin was brought in on mule back. It is not the convenience of the hearse which the people appreciate but the "style."

Like birth, death is an ever present part of the community atmosphere. In this small-scale, traditional setting most of the people who die are old. Of these, most die slowly in their beds. Their close friends and relatives share the last days, old feuds are forgotten and people who haven't spoken to one another for years choose these last days to speak again.

The wake which begins at death is a time for quiet talk, not for cathartic displays of grief. Following death, the body is washed and dressed and placed in bed. Close family members spend the day preparing the house for the evening when the rest of the mourners will start to come in for the wake. Since some people will be at the wake all night long, adult members of the immediate family and a few close friends will probably stay awake the entire time. Unless the deceased was a very special person, most people go to the wake to accompany a friend in his or her sorrow for the passing of a relative. At the wake the men and women sit apart quietly talking with the women occupying the "sitting room" of the house and the men usually sitting in less formal surroundings in front of a kitchen fire. The host, who is normally a close affinal relative, offers cigarettes to the men. Coffee or perhaps liquor may be offered to the mourners, but it is not a central feature of the wake. The body of the deceased lies in his or her bedroom, at times completely unaccompanied. The closest relatives may take turns sitting with the deceased, and at times, other relatives may look in for a brief instant, but no more. In the rooms below, discussion of the deceased is neither a taboo subject, nor the only topic of conversation. A few references to the deceased will be made from time to time, but ordinarily the conversation is the everyday talk of farmers and townsmen. Loud joking is forbidden, but among the men a whispered joke or two may pass.

During the normal course of the evening the men, as they socialize in the bars or meet on the street, make informal dates to go to the wake. "Juan's grandmother, María, finally died. Did you hear the bells? They rang the bell when she died. I'm going to the wake about eleven." Juan's friends will come and stay for several hours at a time. If Juan is a prominent man with client-like relations, these people will come out of respect for Juan. If Juan is a farm laborer or an apprentice or simply a common man, his patrons will often stop by, but only for a few moments. The more important or the more loved the deceased or his relatives, the greater the number of people who will come to the wake. Women leave small children in the care of grandmothers or neighbors and are more inclined to go for kinship or friendship reasons than other types of social relationships.

At mid-morning of the day after the death, the burial begins. Municipal ordinances stipulate that interment begin at least twenty-four hours after the death, but mid-morning or mid-afternoon, if the morning is already taken, are the standard times for burial. As the church bells ring, the coffin is escorted from the home by the priest. The altar boy leads the procession with the large silver cross. Behind him come the priest and subchanter in their robes, then the coffin, the family and the mourners. The women stay at home, and the escort takes the coffin to the church. Waiting at the church are more mourners, including many people who felt so distant that they did not even go to the wake.

As in all such rituals, the rite is always the same but always intangibly different. On February 13, there were two funerals in Almonaster. The first was from the far end of town. Outside the house many men talked and waited. They were all dressed up in dark wool suits and white shirts, all of the buttons buttoned but no neckties, in the "style of the country." The older men, fearing the chill of February, are wearing their overcoats. There is a light air to their attitude, the sun shines bright on the white walls making this sheltered corner very warm in spite of the overall coldness of the day.

The arrival of the priest and the subchanter brings the reality of the occasion to consciousness. A solemn air descends. The men group more formally around the door of the house, making an aisle in the direction of the church. The hearse is parked nearby, but it won't be used. It will simply follow the procession because the men want to carry this old lady to the church. Very quietly the women leave the house in small groups. The moment of separation has come. The coffin is brought to the doorway to be blessed before it goes to the church. Inside the house a woman is sobbing, repeating softly as the coffin is lifted, *"Adios, mamaita, adios."*

The procession begins, but the women don't follow. No one has heard what everyone has heard. She was a very special old woman, very nice, never sick. The priest had said that she began to die on the 23rd of December and now she is finally gone. Everyone is moved. The sorrow is always there, but it is seldom heard. It is always shared in silence. This time, however, was different. From that time on through the next funeral, the men talked often about death. Not about the fear and pain and sorrow but about the inevitability; rationalizing their unspoken hope for personal bravery into strength itself.

After the church service the men alone bear the coffin to the cemetery. They each carry the coffin a few yards. As the cemetery bell rings, the coffin is placed in its niche. The hearse driver, who is also the graveyard keeper, begins immediately to brick up the opening. If it had been an underground burial, hired men would have begun immediately to fill in the grave. Then the mourners break into small groups, some stopping to see niches and graves, some leaving directly. The "burial" is not yet over. Back in town all of the mourners pass by the doorway of the bereaved family. They shake hands with the head of the house and give a short, formal condolence. He thanks each of them in turn.

Even the least religious man goes to funerals. All have the same phrase in mind. *"Ahora pá ti, mañana pá mi,"* "today for you, tomorrow for me." This is not a simple fear of death, nor simply an expression of duties which develop out of specific relationships within the community. It is an expression of each person's membership in the community, of the corporate responsibility of each person to the next. Even the sorriest, most marginal person in the town will have his mourners and will not lack for pallbearers.

The duties, respect, and friendships which develop out of specific relationships are seen in the burials of people from other communities within the multicommunity. Many of these communities use the church and graveyard of Almonaster. The processions follow the same route through the heart of town. When townsmen take part in these funerals, their presence indicates that the deceased or one of his very close relatives is an important or well-known man in the town. To be honored thus, the deceased must have been either economically important or an exceptional human being. Many aldea funeral processions wind through the town causing only a moment's silence in the bars as they pass.

Death has lasting effects on the living, especially on the close relatives of the deceased. Aside from the obvious shifts in family composition, there are the ongoing obligations and proscriptions of mourning. These include the wearing of black, abstention from the use of jewelry and bright colors, and from singing and dancing. In addition, attendance at festivities and entertainments is also proscribed during mourning. The exact term of mourning is dictated by the Catholic church. There is a specific term for each possible relative; the closer the relative, the longer the time of mourning. Most adults over thirty-five or forty years of age will spend large parts of their lives in intermittent periods of mourning of up to several years' duration. This is due to deaths in their own and their parents' generation. These same deaths cause shorter periods of mourning for younger people to whom the deceased stood as aunts and uncles and grandparents.

While the anniversary of a death may be commemorated by the family for several years through masses and prayer services, the normal practice is to commemorate all of the family's deaths on the same day of the year. *Todos Santos,* All Saints Day on November first, is the time officially set aside for individual and community homage to the dead. The cemetery is carefully groomed for this occasion both by the keeper and by the families. Candles, flowers, icons as well as all manner of modern commemorative devices such as battery-lit lanterns and plastic crucifixes decorate the individual graves. A Todos Santos mass is said in the cemetery chapel, and the town in its finery attends. All day long, people visit the cemetery to pay their respects to near and distant relatives.

SOME VALUES AND PATTERNS OF BEHAVIOR

Among the values and patterns of behavior associated with the life cycle can be found elements which are integral to the dynamics of community life and culture. One cluster of elements includes those values and beliefs which are considered hallmarks of community membership. In Almonaster, a person is Catholic and *formal* at the very least. In addition a person's performance in human interaction is patterned in culture specific ways, which is another outward indicator of membership in local culture and society. While the normative value structure underlies most behavior patterns, it often does so in a complex way.

The normative value structure is a generalized, ideal, system whose application to real life situations is colored by each individual's conscious and unconscious goals and knowledge not only of basic values, but also of the underlying beliefs which generate the value system. This complexity is engendered by the *ideal* nature of the value system. Thus, under the central value of formalidad, which can be defined as "following all normative values and sanctions," is found a descending array of more specific values and beliefs. While each of these more specific concepts may be seen as a logical extension of formalidad, they can be contradictory when *applied* simultaneously. Because the set of values employed in any one action may, in fact, be contradictory in that specific context, patterned behavior is often the result of the interaction of contextually opposed values and the basic beliefs by which the social actor evaluates the situation.

For example, a basic tendency toward corporateness or at least a belief in the corporate nature of the community seems implicit in both the virtue of being pueblerino, "having pride in and working for the positive image of one's community," and the "vice" of poison-pen letter writing. Even if similarity of casuality were not assured, the value of being pueblerino conflicts in life with the implicit belief in the coporate control of connubium rights. In the case of suitors from outside the multicommunity the actual behavior, a specific violation of the pueblerino value, is a function of all of these counterpoised factors. Another example results from the belief in the inherent tendency to maximize. To *aprovecharse,* "to take advantage of," is a positive sanction which is opposed by a series of negative beliefs and sanctions, depending on the area of life one considers. Certainly a man's official sexual role is a negative aspect of the basic belief in maximization and a close relative of aprovecharse. The confrontation of this value with the reality of interpersonal relations and the paramount virtue of formalidad, creates the judgmental basis for behavior. Men avoid the intersexual situations which juxtapose these conflicting values or rationalize their " inappropriate" behavior once in the situation with other beliefs and arguments.

Thus the stressed and changing environment with which culture must deal in order to maintain itself and society is not only a function of a adherence to the dictates of a normative value structure, but also of the ambiguities which often occur when the system of values and beliefs is put into practice. Consequently the relationship between culture and behavior is a circular one and this analysis of the rituals of the life cycle has indicated only a few of the complexities of social life which result when values and beliefs are applied to social, economic and political contexts. However incomplete, this analysis of the rites of passage has given enough of an outline of basic community culture and the paramount virtue of formalidad for the discussion of community and multicommunity dynamics to proceed to the rites of the annual cycle which follow in the next chapters.

NOTES

[1]Because there is only one priest for most of the término, other communities must schedule their First Communion services on Sundays after Corpus.

One would not consider taking First Communion in any community other than one's own.

[2]Certain jural aspects of adulthood, such as the vote for both local and national purposes, are not conferred upon the individual until he has married and/or set up an independent household.

[3]Rarely, if ever, does a boy choose to enlist in the armed services which would induct him at an earlier age than those drafted. The boys want to go, but at the appropriate time, not before.

[4]This is close to but not the same as Pitt-River's Honor y Vergüenza (1961 and Peristiany 1966). In Almonaster these terms are not used commonly. (Except Vergüenza which is used in connection with children and pets—almost as a term of endearment.) In part, the difference may be due to the distinction between "real" and "ideal" images. The "ideal" image, very close to Pitt-Rivers' characterization for men, is called being "muy Flamenco." An admired state, it is considered impossible in the community context except perhaps for the Señorito, the dominant, highest status, patron of the town. Otherwise, the "real" image which is both sanctioned and adopted is that of *Formalidad* (closer to Pitt-Rivers's concept of Vergüenza but for both men and women, 1961).

[5]See Appendix 4 for statistics on community exogamy.

[6]Wearing a necktie is not a universal adjunct of being "dressed up." The majority of men do not usually wear ties even when they are dressed up; they simply button the top button of the white shirt. Ties are more common in larger, more "progressive," communities.

A view of Almonaster in winter from the mountain San Cristóbal. The castle and bullring are at the upper left, the church at the center right.

An aldea lies at the edge of a cultivated valley. The houses are found on both sides of one long "street."

A first communicant poses in a sailor suit by the side of the Great Door of the church.

A first communicant with rosary and prayerbook.

Rites and Rituals

SECTION II

The previous description of some of the basic values and beliefs associated with the major rites of passage in Almonaster illustrates at least one important fact: when the system of values and beliefs is applied to current situations, the observed behavior is often a product of the conflict between various parts of that system. The presence of ambiguity or even conflict between different parts of a system of beliefs and values is not uncommon because most ideological systems are not perfectly integrated.

The effects of this intrinsic ambiguity and conflict are not confined, however, to the level of ideology; they often emerge as personal and interpersonal tension. This tension, sometimes in the form of actual hostility, effects the social group negatively, moving it toward disintegration at an ever increasing rate. Although a system of social organization may be capable of organizing, mobilizing and directing complex economic, political and social activities, it is usually not able to eliminate this ambiguity and conflict. Thus there is a constant and pressing need for an institutionalized mechanism for the salutory release of tension and for the reification of group identity and structure which has the potential for reintegrating the group. In Almonaster the cycle of annual rituals, particularly certain of the major yearly festivals, provides just such a mechanism.

The tensions and hostilities engendered by individual movement through social and economic life for Alumñenses are a form of energy which can be released and channeled toward the positive end of the reification of group identity and goals, and hence to the reintegration of the group. Through these group functions, the rituals perform a series of related tasks. They not only reinculcate a perception of each individual's own group and of that person's membership in it, they also reify the social, structural, and physical dimensions of all community groups through each group's own rituals. This ritual reification of the group serves to recreate and institutionalize the boundaries between communities, boundaries which are indispensable in the organization of the multicommunity.

In the beginning of Rites and Rituals Section I, it was stated that since the rites of the annual cycle are those which reaffirm the desired state of an entire group they constitute a dynamic process which consequently may mean many different things at different times and to different people. At the same time, so complex a cultural event inevitably has many secondary functions besides reaffirming group identity and structure. In this chapter and the next, the description and analysis will center only on the ritual processes which produce these crucial group functions. Consequently only the three most important yearly festivals will be considered because unlike the other rituals of the year and many of the secondary functions of the festivals that will be analyzed,[1] these three important yearly rituals alone form the subsystem within the annual cycle of rituals which is able to serve the crucial group functions in the most complete manner.

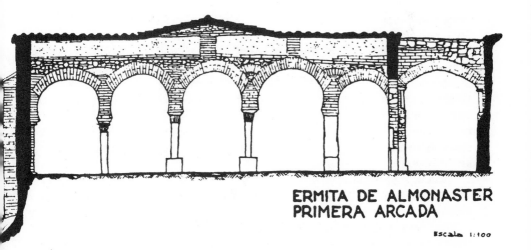

ERMITA DE ALMONASTER
PRIMERA ARCADA

Escala 1:100

CHAPTER 3

Catholic Ritual and Folk Religion: The Functions of a Festival Cycle

In Almonaster, Catholic ritual and folk religion exist side-by-side and form a functionally interrelated system. Except in the lone opinion of the local priest, the people of the area believe that they have one coherent religious tradition, not two. Within the town of Almonaster, which is the most complex community in the multicommunity system, three festivals form an extremely important religious cycle, both within and apart from the cycle of the other annual rituals. Only the sum of the rituals making up this three-festival cycle, rather than any one alone, can succeed in fulfilling the functional mission of releasing social tensions and reintegrating the community.

Although this chapter concentrates on Almonaster, the next chapter investigates the same process in the less complex atmosphere of the aldeas.

The three major festivals which make up the cycle are Semana Santa (Easter Week); The Crosses of May (Invention of the Cross, May third); and the Romería de Santa Eulalia (Pilgrimage of Santa Eulalia of

Mérida, third weekend in May). These three festivals describe a cycle which is activated during about seven weeks, from the beginning of April to the end of May. Each of the festivals serves as a step in the development of group corporateness by heightening the sense of community identity and integration. Because each of the component rituals produces an increasingly higher level of integration until finally an all inclusive level is reached in the third festival, the community as a whole emerges from the rituals as a single corporate group.

The first festival, Semana Santa, "Holy Week," reifies the fact of the basic cultural similarity of all the people of the town, demonstrating the basis for their shared understanding of the specific attributes of community culture. The second festival, The Crosses of May, reifies the physical and social existence of the community as a bounded entity. This is achieved by a first level of integration which results from the creation of two very conscious corporate ritual groups which between them equally partition the space and society of the community. The final festival, Santa Eulalia, reifies the basic unity and harmony of that bounded entity by reasserting the organic interdependence of all of the members of the community. This is a second level of integration which accompanies the ritual formation of a single corporate group out of the personnel of the lower duality. Each festival builds on the foundation provided by the previous rituals. The final state is the one which must endure until the cycle is reactivated during the following Easter (See Table 3–1).

The feelings or response which each stage of this festival cycle elicit in the members of the community are not ones which may be kindled in a moment. They are great social and religious feelings intimately tied to the fundamental identity of the community. Thus the cycle could not truly create these feelings; rather it can only recreate, reawaken these basic characteristics. Because the channeling of energy into the physical and emotional preparations that lead up to the rituals ensures, as do the group activities of the rituals themselves, that people are participating in a highly charged individual state and group atmosphere which leaves no participant untouched by the depth of social and ideological meaning and emotion aroused, the festival cycle serves as a check upon those social conflicts which might be harmful to the community and to reenforce the elemental strength of the corporate bond.

ON THE ORGANIZATION OF
FESTIVALS AND BROTHERHOODS

Two closely related factors influence the functions which a particular ritual may fulfill. The first factor is the organizational principle by which

TABLE 3–1　The Major Festival Cycle
of the Community of Almonaster

	Semana Santa	The Crosses	Santa Eulalia
Church position on the ritual	Sanctioned	Not sanctioned	Sanctioned
Organizational principle	Catholicity	Two brother-hoods or sodalities	One brother-hood
Formal participation in direction of organization	The Priest with informal economic backing of certain rich women	Commoners	Rich
Formal participation in the ritual	Rich and Commoners	Commoners and Rich	Rich and Commoners
Nature of Formal Ritual	Processions and Commun-ion	Processions and dances and other secular fes-tivities	Procession group bull-fight and other secular festivities
Major Function	Cultural Unity: Ex-pression of basic shared understanding and expecta-tion through mass partici-pation as equal indi-viduals.	Social Identity: Two first level groups each with sense of phy-sical and so-cial boundary and unity.	Social Unity: One second level group through uni-fication of first level groups. Com-munity sense of physical and social boundary and unity.
Style of Integration or Solidarity expressed in the festival	Mechanical, if any.	Explicitly mechanical.	Implicitly organic.

the personnel of the ritual are recruited and through which their labors are channeled in terms of both preparation and participation. The other factor is the socioeconomic background of the participants and the extent of their participation in these organizations. A look at Table 3-1 will make these characteristics more comprehensible. Semana Santa is, for example, particularly unsuited to the task of defining groups of people. In an area where everyone is Catholic, the organization, by the fact of common religion, is unable to create boundaries. Such a ritual is, however, quite able to reaffirm the "basic" cultural similarity between individuals.

Similarly the opposition of two separate, but equal, voluntary associations as in the Crosses of May is particularly well suited to the formation of groups and a consciousness of social and physical boundaries. At the same time such associations are very effective for the marshaling of the labor and resources needed to prepare and perform the ritual. Because the rival organizations in the Crosses are directed by hierarchies of common people rather than rich ones, an attitude of egalitarianism characterizes both the internal composition of the two associations and the general style of this festival. This arrangement contrasts markedly from the "directors" of the single brotherhood of Santa Eulalia. Since Santa Eulalia reaffirms the organic solidarity, unity, and integration of the community, its function is to supersede the highly competitive activities and partisan passions of the Crosses. Thus its leaders come from a different and higher social sector than do those of the Crosses.

Before considering each festival in detail, it is important to touch on another general consideration. This is the organization of sodalities. These particular voluntary associations are called *hermandades*, "Brotherhoods." As an organizational principle, Brotherhoods are quite common throughout the multicommunity, as they are in Spain as a whole. It is necessary to consider the basic organization of an hermandad apart from the ritual it performs, since so much of the organization functions behind the scenes.

The bulk of the membership, commonly called *socios* or *hermanos*, comprises the bottom of the organizational pyramid. Above this group is a body of officers, the *Directiva* or *Comisión*. The actual titles of the officers may vary, but they are commonly headed by a *presidente* or *hermano mayor*. In most cases there are several *consejales*, "counselors" or *vocales* who may advise the president or may actively govern with him. Other members of the directiva may hold such offices as vice president, treasurer and secretary. One important characteristic of the directiva is that its members normally serve for an indeterminate term. They are rarely elected; rather they are usually appointed by their predecessors. Normally, the hermano mayor and the secretary or the treasurer are the leaders who deal with the everyday economic tasks of the hermandad. The remaining members of the *directiva* have only two real tasks. They must ensure that the ritual follows the proper course and choose a *Mayordomo*. The *Mayordomo* is the titular head of the year's festivities. He usually serves along with a *Mayordoma* for a one-year term. The *Mayordomos* are the most "visible" of the officers of the hermandad. They not only contribute a great deal of money to the ritual, but also usually lead many parts of it. While the Mayordomos lead the rituals, they often have to rely upon someone on the directiva to tell them how and what to do.

In certain smaller hermandades, which are the subject of the next chapter, this Mayordomo role is taken by a group of men who form a yearly directiva or comisión. They are the figureheads, fund raisers and major contributors who must rely on older, ritually knowledgeable people during the actual ritual. This reliance by Mayordomo, or yearly directiva, on the ritually knowledgeable is not as great as it might be since everyone in the hermandad is normally quite familiar with the general course of the ritual. The knowledgeable opinion is only needed on occasion during the ritual for finer details.

In terms of the analysis of the ritual performances and their effect upon the Almuñenses, the specific features of formal hermandad organization are of secondary importance to the actual festivals and their overall meaning. The wider social significance of the roles of these officers is more apparent in terms of status and prestige than in the ongoing maintenance of group integration. As symbols, the officers stand as only one form among many for the reification of the structural and ideological statements which are the meaning of the rituals. It is important that the key ritual roles be filled, but the actual personality filling it is of less importance. Each ritual represents a complex formula in which there are certain important human and nonhuman elements. Thus the common ritual element of sky rockets is just as important as the office of Mayordomo to the proper presentation of the ritual. Such an arrangement does not denigrate the motives of the "visible" officers (carrying out the office usually represents a very real sacrifice and true dedication); rather it simply points out their relative importance in the context of the rituals themselves.

In summary, the characteristics of the organizational arrangements used in the performance of a yearly cycle of festivals in Almonaster is directly related to the conflicts inherent in an economic system that ranges from subsistence farming to successful latifundia; a system in which formalidad is the most important virtue. The cycle reaffirms beliefs and identities, but it also serves as an "escape valve" which dissipates tension and hostility. Thus the particular persons filling leadership positions and their style of leadership must always be subordinate to the group performance of each ritual for the cycle to succeed in this mission. The genuine success of this cycle of rituals is apparent in the virtual absence of any evidence of *expressed* tension or hostility in Almonaster outside of the festival period.

SEMANA SANTA: FESTIVAL OF THE CHURCH

Semana Santa is a movable holiday which may fall any time between the last week in March and the third week in April. The optimum timing from the Almuñense point of view is any time up to the first week in April. In the last twenty-five years (1946 to 1970), Semana Santa has ended on or before the tenth of April on fifteen occasions. This means that for these years the festival cycle could proceed strictly according to the pattern. During the ten years when the date of Easter is later than the tenth of April, certain minor adjustments must be made in order to complete the cycle on schedule. These adjustments include starting the preparation for the ritual of the Crosses before the Semana Santa ritual has ended. Although this is necessary on the average of two times in every five years, it is always seen as an exceptional step to take rather than as a variant of the standard practice. Strictly speaking it is quite improper, from the Almuñense view, to have rituals overlap. There should always be a simple linear progress from one to the next.

The rituals of Semana Santa last more than a week. They commence on the Saturday before Palm Sunday and continue through Holy Week to Easter Sunday. After Easter Sunday, the ritual continues in slightly attenuated form for two more days. Like all good rites in Almonaster, this one begins with religious rituals which are public, participated in by all, and ends with secular, less rigidly stylized, family-oriented eating. Of particular concern here are the events on the Saturday before Palm Sunday, Holy Wednesday, Thursday and Friday and finally Easter Sunday itself.

Carrying El Señor

Semana Santa in the Christian world is the commemoration of the passion of Christ. This of course is true in Almonaster. But in Almonaster it is not simply Christ, *El Señor,* in the abstract who is the main character in the ritual. *Nuestro Señor de Humildad y Paciencia,* "Our Lord of Humility and Patience," is the particular image of Christ which the people are venerating. On the western margin of the town is the *ermita,* "rural chapel," of this image of Christ. During the year he is found here in the ermita, but for Semana Santa he is brought into the town. On the Saturday before Holy Week, Christ is brought into town. This is called either "Carrying El Señor," or "Going for El Señor."

El Señor de Humildad y Paciencia, is a slightly larger than life-size image of Christ. He is seated in a "Thinker"-like pose. In the town's eyes he is one of the two most important images in all of the término of Almonaster. All year long people visit the ermita to light candles and make offerings, to ask for help and to make pledges. The passion is more tangible for Almonaster because it is the passion of this familiar image. People say that "If you want to see all of the people of the town together in the same place for a moment, all you have to do is go for El Señor. Everyone goes to the ermita. It is the only time when the whole town is in the street at the same time." While the Semana Santa ritual does not create a group, it is a highly emotional, very central experience for all of the people. The offerings, the pleas for help and the pledges are part of the contract which bind many people to El Señor in a very personal dyadic relationship. *Llevando El Señor* is a time for many to make new pledges or to fulfill old ones by *llevando,* "carrying," El Señor from the ermita to the church.

The ermita of El Señor sits by the intersection of the main hardtop road and the long gravel street which forms the entrance to the town from the west. The ermita faces up hill and a bank in front of it forms a natural gallery where many people can gather and see in through the ornamental iron and glass door to the image in the rear. At about seven-thirty in the evening of the Saturday before Palm Sunday people begin to gather on this bank. By eight-fifteen, about two hundred people are present. The mood is mildly religious. Everyone is talking at once but in hushed tones. The conversation ranges from experiences of being helped by El Señor, to the unusual number of candles which are burning in the ermita, to sports, politics and business. Everyone is suddenly aware of the altar boy hurrying up with the key to the ermita. Such keys are always in the custody of the particularly devout women who take charge of religious duties like the maintenance of ermitas. Just behind the boy with the key come the subchanter, the second altar boy, and the priest himself.

The priest passes the word to start the people walking in two parallel lines back toward town. It takes a while because no one wants to start before they see El Señor come out of the ermita. The two altar boys, one with the cross and the other with the incensor, wait in the middle of the street a few steps ahead of the crowd. The subchanter has taken the key and hurried into the ermita. The *paso* ("litter," in the ritual context only) of El Señor has been prepared ahead of time, but last minute details must be taken care of. With the subchanter are six or eight men and older boys. The ornate candelabra which is part of the paso must be lit and the paso itself, which sits on shrouded saw-horses, must be eased away from the wall and lifted onto the shoulders of the first carriers. The back of the ermita is narrow and the flowers and candelabra shake and sway precariously as the paso is lifted. "First to the height of your arms," directs the subchanter. He is the *capataz*, "foreman," of the paso. He leads the paso out of the ermita. Outside the men lift the paso at his command, "Now, to the shoulder!" Borne on the shoulders of six men, El Señor is ready to go into town. The two lines of escort begin to walk slowly toward the first light on the edge of the town.

The head of the line is made up of children, then come women and finally men. Near the end of the lines, in the middle of the street, walks the group of men who carry the paso, behind them the rest of the men and older boys who want to have a turn carrying. In the middle walks the priest reciting and singing. The people sing along with the priest, the common Spanish church songs which the children always seem to know best. Those who do not sing, walk silently in reverence. Every fifty yards or so the subchanter stops the paso by knocking with a brass door-knocker which is attached to the front of the paso. Each carrier has a staff with a "y"-shaped end. The knock is the signal to stop and then, all together, to lower the paso so that each of the six handles is supported by one of the staves. At each stop new men ask to be allowed to carry the paso and most of the carriers turn over their places to someone else. One or two of the carriers have pledged to carry the paso the entire way. After a few seconds the subchanter knocks again; they lift the paso and go on.

For almost an hour the paso moves through the town, El Señor surrounded by candles and red carnations. The course of the procession goes to the central plaza and then directly to the church on the western side of town. As the lines reach the door of the church the people enter and stand in front of the benches, the children in front, then the women and finally the men. In keeping with the personal style of the procession, El Señor comes in through the side door that the people have used. On more "official" occasions the Puerta Mayor, the "great door" is used for the entrance and exit of processions and images. El Señor is brought to the altar and set to the right of the congregation. All of the crosses are shrouded for Easter, and El Señor with his look of benevolent anguish, dominates the front of the church.

Many of the youths and men who have followed and carried the paso do not enter the church. About 175 people are inside for the first of five prayer and sermon sessions which make up a *quinario*. If the first sermon is particularly interesting, many people will attend on the next four nights, but normally the sermon is predictable and attendance drops off quickly to 50 or 60. In this ritual, what seems to matter is the actual bringing of El Señor to the church, not listening to the familiar religious service.

In contrast to the emotional commitment which brings everyone out to "go for El Señor," the Palm Sunday service and procession only attract those with free time. For merchants, professionals, rich people, old people and adolescents, Palm Sunday and the short procession seem to be more of a pageant than a religious experience. Most of the people of the night before are busy in their gardens on this morning. The "traditionalists" who prefer the early mass and those who must put free Sunday time to productive use, go to mass at eight-thirty. The procession is held during the eleven o'clock mass. In their best clothes, carrying olive and palm branches, the congregation follows the priest out of the church for a two block procession, which never reaches any of the civil or religious symbols of the community.

While other parts of Spain have religious rituals which go on during the entire Holy Week, Almonaster leaves Monday, Tuesday and Wednesday relatively ritual free. The only unusual events are the presence of a "missionary" sent out from Sevilla, and the evening *Quinario* services in the church. If this missionary is exceptional, he may increase the attendance at these functions, but this is rare. Confident of their faith, few Almuñenses feel that their Catholicism is so weak that they need to hear the preaching of a missionary.

Confession and Communion

One of the most powerful of the Semana Santa experiences takes place on Wednesday and is really preparation for the Thursday evening mass which celebrates the Last Supper. This experience is a profoundly moving experience for most of the men and many of the women in town. On Wednesday all but a few wage laborers take part of the day off to confess. There are so many people who desire to make their confession that the missionary hears them in the chapel on the central plaza while the priest hears confessions in the church.

The central plaza and the *placeta* next to the church are full of people all afternoon. Women and children tend to move purposefully around the plaza, the men rather aimlessly. Standing in groups, men salute each newcomer, and move from one group to the next talking and joking. Almost without exception, the men are nervous. Their anxiety shows in laughter at poor jokes or at nothing at all. Most of the men freely admit that they only confess once a year and that they don't like it at all. "It is even worse for some people in the countryside where they may not confess every year. They have a drink or two before they go and the priest can smell it on their breath and gets angry with them." It is not the actual need to confess all of their sins which upsets the men nor the fear of being revealed in some way. "You never 'tell' the priest anything. He will ask you questions. You answer 'yes' or 'no'." The priest learns very little about each man since the standard questions are neither threatening nor revealing. The threatening part of confession is the unaccustomed act itself.

The *Jueves Santo,* Holy Thursday, ritual begins at six-thirty in the evening with the ringing of the church bells calling the town to mass at seven. Everyone stops work early to be ready for this service. By seven the church is as full as it can get. Many people are standing for lack of bench space. In front of the first pews are set twelve high-backed chairs. Here sit twelve respected men of the town. Normally these are men from the Town Council and include the Alcalde, "Mayor," and other respected, though not necessarily rich, men.

The high point of the service is the taking of communion. At any other mass only a few people actually take communion. Usually these persons rise at random from the congregation, first from the women's and children's section and then from the men's. The communion on Jueves Santo is quite different. First the twelve men take communion and then the entire congregation follows row by row. By the time the first men from the back of the church start down the center aisle, all of the women and children and the twelve important men are again seated and watching. In a sense, no one notices who takes communion at this time. The ones who are noticed, who are commented upon, are those who *don't* take communion, "If they see you do it they may or may not notice. If they don't see you, then they begin to talk. 'What kind of man is this? He says that he is a Catholic, but how does he act on Jueves Santo, he didn't take communion!' It is always better to do it right, than to give them cause to talk."

In terms of the major functions of the Semana Santa ritual, this act of communion on Jueves Santo epitomizes the reification of cultural membership. The similarity in cultural terms is uppermost at this moment. "What kind of Catholic is he?" is the question they ask of someone who misses this ritual. Not what kind of Almuñense or Andalucian or even Spaniard. Sociological distinctions, group membership, values generated by social groups, none of these are important here. Catholicism is taken by Almuñenses (and indeed the majority of Spaniards) to be a basic fact of their universe. Given that a person is a passable Spanish speaker, that is, not obviously African or Northern European by language, it would never occur to anyone to question the fact that he is Catholic.

This attitude is very close to the governmental propaganda of Spain which says that, being a good Catholic is synonymous with being a good Spaniard. In the Almonaster context it is not enough simply to take communion sometime during the year. It must be done at this time. For those who are unable to attend on Jueves Santo, there is a special public communion service after the service on Viernes Santo, Holy Friday. The "official" or formal liturgy for this church service on Friday does not include communion. As the service ends the priest announces that there will be a special communion for those who couldn't come the day before. Rather than leave, the entire congregation remains seated while the few who missed the ritual are given communion.

After Jueves Santo mass each family goes home for dinner. Before dinner they eat a special confection similar to French toast called *torrija* that is eaten only on this occasion. Though a festive family occasion, the people do not linger over dinner. At ten o'clock the bells will ring again for the Jueves Santo procession.

Following a common Andalucian pattern for Semana Santa processions, the Jueves Santo procession has two pasos. The first one in the line of march supports an image of Christ. Following at some distance is a more elaborate paso with an image of the Virgin. On Jueves Santo in Almonaster the image of Christ is the same one that was brought from the ermita almost a week before. The image of the Virgen de Gracia follows on a paso covered with lit candles. The full-size image is clothed in flowing robes and above it is a velvet canopy. During the beginning of Semana Santa, the image of the Virgin is set amid tiers of candles at the front of the church, but when the people arrive for the procession, she is already set on her paso.

With most of the town outside the Puerta Mayor waiting to parade beside the two sacred pasos, the two "foremen" engineer the *salida,* the ritual exit of the images from the Church. Along with the first set of carriers and a dozen more willing helpers, they guide the pasos out of the great door. El Señor passes easily. His paso is comparatively light and compact. The Virgen de Gracia not only weighs more, but her greater height and swaying canopy make her top-heavy. Very carefully she is eased out of the great door. She emerges into the procession. El Señor is ahead, between two lines of children. Walking between the lines, behind El Señor, is a knot of men and boys who wish to carry the paso. Further back between the lines of men comes the Virgin. In addition to the knot of extra carriers, each paso has a Guardia Civil escort in dress uniform and machine guns

The route, though longer than the one on Palm Sunday, is also devoid of ritual stations. While symbolically covering the town, the procession manages to pass through the central square without passing in front of, or taking note of, the ayuntamiento, the seat of secular authority. The same is true for both of the monumental crosses. This contrasts with the processional route on the First Communion/Corpus Christi, and especially with the Crosses ritual processions which come next in the cycle. Along the route at a few intersections, in the plazas and on balconies, the spectators watch. Most of the town is walking in the procession, the audience is made up of the aged and infirm, as well as the very young. The mood is deeply reflective. Even after the *regreso*, "return to the church," the people are quiet. Many who would normally be the most boistrous carry one or both of the pasos. Some, for the first time, are big enough to participate. It is a ritual duty and an honor for men. Others carry the pasos in order to fulfill a pledge to the diety. Still others carry it before the diety fulfills his part of the bargain, showing their good faith and hopefully ensuring that their pleas will be heard and acted upon. Whatever reason, honor or pledge, many have a great deal to think about.

As in most of Semana Santa, the following day proceeds with no special events until the evening. The Good Friday service begins at seven. All Catholics again participate in this important part of the ritual. Since the beginning of Lent all of the crucifixes have been covered, but at this service, the cross is ritually uncovered. Once the actual uncovering is accomplished, all in turn go up to the steps of the altar where each makes a monetary offering and kisses a large crucifix held by two altar boys. Following this act of devotion and the special communion for those who could not take communion on Jueves Santo, the members of the congregation return to their homes for dinner.

As on the previous evening there is a procession following the same route. The only variation is in the pasos themselves. El Señor does not lead the procession. For this evening there is a larger than life-sized cross and crucified Christ. He is carried horizontally, feet first by three bearers.

This is the last Semana Santa procession if one discounts, for the moment, the return of El Señor to his ermita on the Monday after Easter. The procession ends at about eleven and the church is soon empty of all but two or three shadowy figures. Rapidly they go about the business of dismantling the paso of the Virgin, and returning her and the Crucified Christ to their accustomed niches in the walls of the church. Because waiting on Christ or the Virgin is no longer the honor it was during the procession, these workers have to be paid for their labors by one of the rich families which is known for its piety. This same family helps with the decoration of the church and the preparation of the pasos each year. In contrast, other rich families are not as active in official church ritual or works.

On Saturday, at seven in the evening, there is a relatively poorly attended ritual of the Way of the Cross, but by eleven-forty most of the town is present for a long service. Before midnight it is the Saturday mass, and after twelve it becomes the Resurrection Sunday mass. The highlight of this service comes at midnight when Christ is risen. Outside the church a series of rockets is set off. These are the first and last rockets of Semana Santa, but over the next month and a half of this festival cycle there will be hundreds more.

The Gira

Easter Sunday dawns with the beginning of the secular celebration of Easter. This secular celebration, aside from its function as "fun," symbolizes cultural, but *not* social unity. Major rites in Almonaster always end with a secular feast and Semana Santa is no exception. Here the ritual is called a *gira* or "picnic" (in this context only). It must take place outside of town, and in addition, there is the traditional Easter requirement of hardboiled eggs and *roscas*. The eggs are sometimes colored, but this is not a necessity. The *rosca* is a special kind of Easter bread. All during Semana Santa the bakery works extra hours and hires extra help in order to make enough of the anise-flavored rolls. Each person must have at least one of the lopsided, doughnut-shaped rolls. Beyond these basic requisites, the menu includes all manner of cooked and preserved delicacies.

In the early afternoon families begin to leave town by all of its exits. There is no traditional place to have the gira, but most families end up at one of the five or six more notable countryside spots. Some of these are only a few minutes from the town; others are forty-five minutes to an hour away by foot. At some of these favorite spots there may be a large number of families scattered in clusters among the trees. The children run about together. The young adults join the children in circle games and singing. The older people talk and watch. Then after several hours everyone walks back to town for a late afternoon nap.

For most people the return from the gira is the end of Semana Santa. There is still the return of El Señor to the ermita but this lacks the importance of his first trip. The gira is repeated on Monday and Tuesday for the children and some of the older boys and girls will accompany them, but although these weekday picnics are fun outings for the children, they are hardly ritually important for the adults of Almonaster. By Easter Sunday, Semana Santa has done all it can to reify the basic cultural similarity of all of the people in the Almonaster universe. On Easter Sunday, after everyone is up from the after-gira nap, the second part of the festival cycle begins. The formation of the first level groups begins and the two Crosses of May begin to seize the attention of the town.

THE CROSSES: FESTIVAL OF
THE COMMUNITY

In comparison with Semana Santa, the Crosses of May has a quality of richness found in few of the other festivals. The local celebration of the Day of the Cross is considered by the people of the término to be one of the two most noteworthy celebrations of the year. The secular side of the festival is much more highly developed than is the case with local Semana Santa ritual and there is a rich fund of folk literature, in the form of ritual songs, not found in the latter. As a ritual organized and directed by the people themselves, the finer details of ritual and preparation are "common property." Each person's "part" is an active one. Beyond the elaboration of both the sacred and secular parts of the festival, is the important fact that the people realize that this festival, unlike Semana Santa, is peculiar to Almonaster. Coupled with this realization is the strong feeling of pride which Almuñenses have in this festival as, "a thing of *gran mérito.*"

The "great merit" of the Crosses ritual is owed, in part, to the physical symbols of this festival, the monumental crosses themselves. The two crosses stand at opposite sides of town, each in its own plaza. The crosses are made of ornamental iron. Standing about three feet tall, they are each mounted on a square whitewashed pillar about six feet high. These physical symbols have a profound meaning to the people. The statement that "The crosses are the heart of the town" is not an idle metaphor nor a grammatical error. Given that the creation of two very partisan groups is one of the "results" of the festival, the reference to *both* crosses as the "heart" of the town is illustrative of only one of the two levels on which the ritual has to be considered. On the one hand, there is the level of highly partisan "un-religious" behavior, which is a product of the structure and organization of the ritual. This is the level of the sodalities of the crosses. In contrast, the crosses themselves belong to a different level, that of the "official" ideology of the Crosses ritual, which says that a "real *crucero*" ("true follower of the Cross") thinks only in terms of venerating the cross. The conflict between these two levels is quite apparent to the Almuñense.

"What the crosses mean, and the way a good crucero *should* act is one thing; the way people actually do act is another thing altogether." The difference is lamentable, but inevitable, in their eyes. A description of the ritual itself will show that a basic distinction is made between the treatment of the opposite cross and the treatment of the brotherhood of that cross. Both levels are interrelated, but in terms of the ritual cycle, the level of the competetive brotherhoods is the more important.

The two brotherhoods are known officially as, the *Hermandad de la Santa Cruz del Llano* and the *Hermandad de la Santa Cruz de la Fuente*. In every day use these titles are shortened to *El Llano* and *La Fuente*. To the outsider this can create some confusion since each of these terms has several referents. El Llano can refer to the plaza where the cross of that name is; or it can refer to the brotherhood; and it can also refer to the meeting place of that brotherhood. The same is true for La Fuente with the addition that there is actually a fountain near the plaza which is also referred to as La Fuente.

The spatial arrangement of the crosses, El Llano in the east, La Fuente in the west, is used as one of the explanations for the traditional epithets which find the Llano, "the cross of the rich," and the Fuente, "the cross of the poor." Several rich families live between the plaza of the Llano and the nearby church and many belong to the Llano; but commoner members of both groups are quick to point out that this does not create a meaningful difference since not all the rich people belong to the Llano, and they are neither active in the direction of the brotherhoods, nor do they contribute more money than anyone else.

Contradicting the Almuñense explanation of the "rich" and "poor" epithets is the often stated assumption that the hermandades do not represent geographic divisions of the town. When the members of the hermandades are plotted on a map of the town, it is readily apparent that in an *absolute* sense the hermandades do not represent geographic divisions since members of both are found in all parts of town. From the *statistical* point of view, however, the geographic nature of the hermandades is overwhelmingly reaffirmed. While socios of each hermandad are found in all parts of town, the relative number of Llaneros is greater near the Llano than it is near the Fuente. On some streets near the Llano, Llano membership reaches 100 percent. Similarly, near the Fuente, some areas are almost 100 percent for this rival brotherhood.

Closely related to the Almuñense assumption of the *non*-geographic nature of the hermandades are two facts of membership. First, a person may change his hermandad affiliation when he pleases; and second, he may be a member of both hermandades at the same time. These factors of mobility and duality of membership are opposed by the stated value that a good crucero only belongs to one hermandad. The reasons for mobility and duality of membership are not related to the ideology of the Crosses; instead they represent two secondary functions of the ritual. The first deals with dating and general relations between unmarried males and females. This is the function of dances and meetings of the hermandades as places where boys may interact closely with girls. The second deals with the animosity which the hermandades create. Here the problem is primarily an economic one in which people fear that conflicting membership between two people may preclude amicable economic relations.

These three assumptions (single membership preferred, mobility in membership, and duality of membership allowed) and the functional bases for them together describe three possible categories of membership:

1. Those who belong to one hermandad and attend the secular festivities of only one.
2. Those who belong to one hermandad and attend the secular festivities of two.
3. Those who belong to two hermandades and attend the secular festivities of both.

The first category includes all females of any age as well as married men whose economic base does not involve retail selling or similar public relationships. The second category includes unmarried men and boys with strong allegiance to the religious and social duties of their hermandad.

These members, motivated by friendship and the distribution of available girls, will commonly attend the secular festivities of both, except for the final secular festivity when they will feel bound to attend only their own. Mobility, the changing of membership from one to the other, is very rare in these first two categories. The third contains one group which commonly reverts to single membership on marriage. This is a small number of unmarried boys and men who are motivated solely by the availability of girls. They often change after marriage to affiliation with only their wife's hermandad. Men from other categories do not change on marriage across membership lines. Most of the people in the third category are merchants who feel that their business would suffer if they failed to demonstrate their "neutrality" by paying dues to both hermandades and making, at least, token appearances at the secular festivities of both.

The choice between categories clearly indicates a difference between the roles of men and women as members of an hermandad. Women do not have the option of holding dual membership and they should not attend both sets of secular festivities. For men the choice obviously depends on each individual's feeling as to the relative importance of the secular versus the "religious" functions of the hermandades. Significantly, the majority of members are found in the first category, including some merchants and officials who "should" take the position of dual membership but choose not to.

These same considerations effect the amount or style of participation in the sodalities and the actual ritual. All official active participants in the religious ritual are from the first two categories only. They include the women who form the bulk of the religious procession and the few male members of the procession. All office holders, from the yearly Mayordomos up through the president, are from categories 1 and 2, if they are unmarried, but never from category 3. In addition, the higher the economic level, the less active will be the participation of even the most devout members of the hermandad. Rather than be a member of both, such a person becomes a spectator for one. This is not simply due to problems of buying and selling relations. It has its basis in the stricture against the expression of hostility or competition in the patron/client relationship. Active participation by the patron would create real tension and hostility with clients of the opposite hermandad. The result is that merchants, landowners, and important officials are barred from active participation in the hermandad either by their duality of membership or through the inactivity which their passionate devotion to one hermandad necessitates.

The Flowers

Preparation for the Crosses of May begins on Easter Sunday evening with a volley of rockets. There will be a volley of rockets every night at ten-thirty right up until the festival itself. The rockets are a signal that the house of the hermandad is now open and that members should come to assist in the preparations for the festival of the Cross. This is the "reason" for the nightly activity at each of the "club houses." In fact, the normative position on everything the hermandad does is the veneration of the cross; hence these nightly "work" meetings, which are called *Las Flores*, "the flowers."

The actual preparatory activities at Las Flores are of two kinds. There are several hundred paper roses, lilies and daisies to be made. These are for decorating the cross and the pillar it stands on. Secondly, there are songs and musical accompaniment to be learned and practiced. Each part of the rite has its own traditional songs. The singers are accompanied by tamborines and a drum and pipe. During the parades which are the high points of the rite, the girls, who form the parade, are lead by six or eight of their number who play the tamborines. The drum and pipe are played by a special musician, the *tamborilero*. The hermandades each have their own tamborilero. Although they are paid for their playing, they only play for their own brotherhood, never for the other. At Las Flores, the singing is usually accompanied only by the tamborines. It would be too expensive to hire the tamborilero for all of these preparatory meetings.

Any member of the hermandad may come to Las Flores, but in practice only the active members do. This group includes all of the unmarried girls who will march in the parade or *Romero*, the main ritual of the *romería*. The *romería* or "pilgrimage," is the ceremony of the Day of the Cross itself. All of the unmarried boys who will be following the *Romero* are active participants at Las Flores as well as younger girls and boys. Other members may stop in for a moment, but this is rare.

On April nights at about ten-thirty each hermandad fires its rockets and people begin to go to Las Flores. For a while there are only a few people at the small one-room house where the Llano holds its meetings. One of the directiva brings the key to the house and two or three rockets. The Mayordomo and other older boys are waiting. With a cigarette they light off the rockets. They open the house and set up the benches which run around all four walls of the small room. Most of the members are still finishing dinner and many of the girls have to clean up after dinner, so the room fills slowly. While only a handful of children and young adults are present, they all sit together on the same bench and make paper flowers in assembly line fashion. One person cuts out petals, another makes the center of the flower by twisting paper around a slender wire. At the end of the bench are the people who combine the parts, tying the flower off with thread. One of the older girls oversees this process, since the flowers must be just right, but both boys and girls participate. They use the wide tamborines for containers while they make flowers.

When more people arrive, the first group of flower makers splits up; consequently when the room is full, age-mates tend to be sitting together with the boys and girls mixed freely. While a small core of flower makers continue to work, the rest clamor for the tamborines to be given over to their rightful use as musical instruments.

The tamborine is not an easy instrument to play because skill and much practice are necessary before anyone is able to play it for a reasonable length of time. While one or two of the older girls play for the singing, younger girls play along, learning by participation. The older girls, ranging in age from about 16 to 27, can play for over half an hour. Younger girls, even though they may have the sound right and are able to follow the tune, lack the necessary stamina. While only a few boys can play the tamborine (which is never played officially by boys), almost all of them can and do sing all of the songs of the hermandad. There are two styles of song, the *coplas del Romero*, which are used during the parade, the Romero itself, and *fandangos* of the Cross, which are sung before and after the Romero. The *coplas del Romero* are the more religious in theme of the two. During the ceremony itself, each group will air some derisive *coplas*, but these are new from year to year. At Las Flores the old standard *coplas* are sung. The second group, the *fandangos*, have both religious and secular themes among which are songs of courtship and pride in the hermandad.[2] These songs are not only important ritual elements, but also are the main vehicle by which new members are inculcated into ideology of the hermandad.

Overt differences between the hermandades are minor from the point of view of an outsider. The paper flowers are different from one to the other, there is a very minor difference in the rhythm of songs and some of the tunes. On the whole, most of the coplas and fandangos are the same, substituting the name of the hermandad doing the singing. The following three coplas del Romero are sung by both groups and can be heard almost every night of the flowers:

*

En un madero de Cruz
a Jesús crucificaron
y por eso sus hermanos
con devoción la adoramos

*

On the timber of the Cross
they crucified Jesus and
because of this (we) its
brothers with devotion
worship it.

*

Ya vienen las golondrinas
con el vuelo muy sereno
para quitarle las espinas
a Jesús de Nazareno

*

Now come the swallows
with quiet flight to
take out the thorns from
Jesus of Nazareth

*

Somos Ilegando a la Cruz
con el traje de serrana
en homenaje al Señor
y a su sangre derramada
(Coplas del Romero)

*

We are arriving at the
Cross in the dress of
serranas in homage to
the Lord and to his spilt blood.

These coplas and numerous others like them provide the overt reason for the existence of the hermandades. They include explicit parallels between the Biblical actors of the Passion and the roles of the ritual actors in the ceremony of the crosses. The parallel between the swallows of the second copla and the *serranas*, "mountain girls," of the third is not an accident, and similar examples appear below. The relationship between the symbolism of the songs and the actual ritual is a topic unto itself which can only be mentioned here in passing. What is important is that this ideology of religious purpose is countered by equally popular coplas and fandangos which express the more secular functions of the ceremony and of the preparation meetings.

Bendita sea la Cruz,
Bendits sean las flores
y también bendita sean
todas las que se las ponen.
(Copla del Romero)

Blessed be the Cross,
blessed be the flowers
and also blessed be all
of those who place them
(on the cross).

*

Viva el Llano porque tiene

*

Hurray for the Llano because

gracia y sal de Andalucía,
Donde quiera que me vaya
no la olvidaré en la vida.
(Copla del Romero - el Llano)

it has the grace and wit
of Andalucia
No matter where I go
I will never forget it
(the hermandad).

*

De las que están bailando
la que lleva el delantal
es la novia de mi hermano
pronto tengo una cuñá (cuñada).
(Fandango de la Cruz)

Of those who are dancing
the one who is wearing the
apron is the girlfriend of
my brother,
very soon I'll have a
sister-in-law.

*

Viva el Llano que es mi tierra
y San Martín me patrón,
viva la gente del Llano
porque del Llano soy yo.
(Fandango de la Cruz - el Llano)

Hurray for the Llano,
my country,
and Saint Martin my patron,
Hurray for the people of
the Llano
because I'm from the Llano.

After having sung songs of courtship and songs of devotion with equal gusto for about an hour and a half amid talking and joking, some begin to call for *Sevillanas* or *Corro*. Sevillanas are the song and dance form of Sevilla and unlike the Fandangos of the Cross, they are danced to as well as sung. Everyone forms a circle singing and clapping while several couples dance in the middle. This is an activity which appeals most to the older participants. The rest sing along, but at each pause they ask for Corro. Corro is a generic term for circle games. Each game has its own song. These are games suited to the wide age spread present at Las Flores. Almost every night ends with the entire group playing *Gallena Siega*, "the Blind Hen," one of the most popular. The person who is "it," is blindfolded and set in the middle of the circle. All join hands and the rules state that no one must let go. The person who is "it" turns three times around while the circle also turns; then he or she must try to catch someone. Once caught the person must be identified by the "it" using touch only. If the "it" is unsuccessful, then that person continues; if he or she guesses right, then the new person is "it."

These gay and carefree nightly meetings of young people have a profound effect on the people of the town. Everyone is affected, moved either to friendly competition or to tense repressed hostility. In general, relations between hermandades are better at the level of the children and young unmarrieds than on the level of their elders. Normally the competition at the level of Las Flores entails an occasional derisive song and a minor parade and rocket competition on Sunday evenings. The hermandad pays the tamborilero to come to Las Flores where he plays for the singing and sevillanas. During these evenings he also leads the group on a parade through the town. As the marchers go through the darkened streets, they are comparing themselves to the opposition in terms of the quality of their singing, their numbers and the number of rockets which they shoot off. On the level of their elders, the competition has no stylized outlet and can create some real interpersonal problems. Where the young feel the competition in the rather structured setting of Las Flores and the ritual itself, the adults must face it in the context of their normal daily lives. The young occasionally are moved to overt hostile acts, but only after the entire ritual has served to heighten their sense of pride in their identity. In contrast, the attitude of adults seems to be much closer to intergroup hostility.

Inter-hermandad hostility among adults becomes a problem whenever it appears, but particularly when it involves spouses or friends. Although mixed marriages are fairly rare, the stories of their problems are not. Fights over real and imagined slights of a spouse's hermandad sometimes lead to husbands who do their own cooking and laundry or even sleep on the doorstep. Most mixed families soon learn that the only smooth road is one in which they pretend when they are together that nothing out of the ordinary is afoot in town. In these houses, it is taboo to mention anything to do with the Crosses.

Much commoner is the problem which a man faces with his friends, many of whom may be from the other side. Each night of the year he meets with them in the bars of town. The conversation is on many topics, including the general gossip of the town's daily life. The Crosses, Las Flores and the Sunday parades should be a part of this conversation, except for the danger of comparison. Drawing even the most innocent of comparisons will inevitably cause someone to feel that his side has been attacked. He could retaliate with a nasty comment, which could start unwanted escalation. In the average case the need to conform to the rules of formalidad keeps the injured party from saying anything. Instead he walks out of the bar and stops talking to the person who made the comment and perhaps to those to whom the comment was made, depending on how he thinks they reacted to it. Hopefully, he will again speak to them in a few weeks. He certainly won't be speaking to them the next morning. Again, the defense is to avoid the topic in bar conversation.

Bartenders, like store keepers and officials, are meant to be neutral, and they try to stop any conversations they see going in the wrong direction.

The people of Almonaster agree that talk about the Crosses is not for bars; nor for stores, where the same problem exists among women. The solution tends to limit the potential danger of interpersonal ruptures but certainly does not help to quell the developing hostility and competitiveness. The artificial rule against talking about the Crosses only serves to outline more clearly the competitive condition in each person's mind. Try as they may during this time, best friends who are from opposite sides, find it hard not to become estranged. They may still keep the same schedule at night, but as time goes on they are less and less intimate in the bar. Each includes the other less and less in their conversation.

DOMINGO DE CHUBARBA

The pace quickens on the Sunday before the actual Cross of May ceremony. On this Sunday each hermandad holds a major preparatory ritual called the Sunday of *Chubarba* or The Bringing of the *Chubarba*. This ritual marks the beginning of the actual ceremony time. *"Desde la traída de la chubarba a la gira"* ("from the bringing of the chubarba to the picnic"), is a common phrase encompassing the entire festival. Chubarba is a green holly-like plant which is one of the indispensible ritual items used in decorating the Cross. It is a low shrub which grows along the creeks and in low damp places and has a sharp, thorny point at the end of each small laurel-shaped leaf.

At three o'clock on the Sunday afternoon of the chubarba, a volley of rockets is shot off from each of the crosses. The girls and children quickly gather at the base of the cross with their tamborines. As they sing songs of the cross, more rockets are fired and the boys begin to appear. By four there are a large number of people present, all members of the hermandad. The tamborilero has arrived and someone has brought a donkey. The people escort the active members, the older children and unmarried young adults, to the edge of town. The tamborilero leads the group as they all sing and many rockets are fired. Until they are far into the countryside each group will be aware of the other by the rocket explosions. At the town's edge the group goes on alone with its donkey. Each brotherhood has its own traditional picnic spot and a traditional chubarba picking area located on the side of town associated with its cross. The Llano picnic area is about a mile to the east with their chubarba area in the wilder countryside to the south of the picnic spot. The Fuente picnic area is on the west about three-quarters of a mile from town. Their chubarba site is a short distance beyond to the southwest.

Walking in couples, singing songs of the cross, it takes about an hour to get to the chubarba area. The way leads along the gullies and creeks, and the members cut *chubarba* with pen knives as they go. The thorns prick and cut their hands as they collect the chubarba which gives rise, along with the wild asparagus, to many suggestive jokes. When each brotherhood arrives at its chubarba area, it throws down its bunches of the shrub and has a snack of bread and wine and tapas. After this snack, couples used to go off alone to "pick chubarba," but today so many younger children go along with the couples that this is difficult. Instead, while some continue to pick chubarba, "so that the Llano will be sure to bring in a bigger load than the Fuente," the rest dance and play at Corro. As the day wanes, each group loads its donkey with an impressive bundle of *chubarba* and then starts for home. At the edge of town the rest of the hermandad and the tamborilero meet and join their group.

The entry of the chubarba is the first ritual which the two hermandades do not do simultaneously. In this case, the Llano enters first and the Fuente must wait outside the town until their turn comes. At about eight o'clock the majority of the members of the Llano are waiting with the tamborilero on the eastern margin of town on the *Era de la Cuesta*, "the threshing floor of the hill." When the chubarba arrives everyone marches into the town behind the loaded donkey and the tamborilero. Everyone sings and rocket explosions are almost continuous. They go straight to the Santa Cruz del Llano. The parade goes around the cross three times singing to the tamborilero and the tamborines. The rest of the membership is waiting in the Llano, a gathering of perhaps 250 people. After three turns around the cross, they all stand in front of the cross and sing fandangos. The donkey is led off to the house of the hermandad where the chubarba is unloaded. When the rockets indicate that the parade of the Llano is over, the Fuente enters the other side of town in the same manner.

Las Flores continues all during this last week and in the bars the subject is more taboo than ever, as everyone becomes infected with the excitement of the coming festival. On Thursday night only one or two people are allowed to come to the hermandad house and Las Flores is suspended. With the help of some of the older men, usually of the directiva, and the most knowledgeable girls, the actual decorations for the cross are put together. Most important is the covering of a wicker horseshoelike arch with chubarba and paper roses. This arch will frame the cross. The

base of the cross will be covered with chubarba, paper flowers and paintings and tapestries. All these preparations take place in the house and
nothing is actually put on the cross yet; nevertheless all is ready. The
whole hermandad is not invited to this since "they would all get in the
way," "this isn't like Las Flores—we have to get a lot done in a hurry."
By Friday night, the meeting of Las Flores is particularly happy and
noisy since Saturday is the *Dia de Las Flores* and the beginning of three
days of nonstop secular and religious excitement called the Cross of May.

The Cross of May

DAY OF THE FLOWERS

At sunset on Saturday, the *Dia de Las Flores*, each hermandad returns
from its picnic area where it has spent the late afternoon. As in the
Chubarba ceremony of the Sunday before, the rest of the hermandad
awaits them on the outskirts of town. This time each member has a long
branch of poplar. The Llaneros are again the first into the town. They
return from El Venero, their picnic spot in the campo, to the Era de la
Cuesta, where the rest await them. The poplar branches are symbolic of
the wild flowers that they are supposed to pick during the afternoon to
decorate the cross. They don't pick any flowers; instead they adorn the
cross with the paper ones they have been making throughout April.
Spring and efflorescence are important elements of the entire ritual as the
following Copla del Romero indicates:

En primavera florida	In flowery spring
adoramos a la Cruz	we venerate the Cross
y la cubrimos de flores	and cover it with flowers,
de canciones y de luz.	songs and with light.

Among the many coplas that are sung there are a few which are used only
during specific parts of the ritual. These are self-explanatory and they are
often repeated many times during that part of the ritual. The following is
such a copla from the Llano:

En la Santa Cruz del Llano	In the sainted Cross of

ponemos nuestros amores	the Llano
y la cubrimos de ramos	we put our love
en la tarde de las flores.	and we cover it with
	branches
	on the afternoon of the
	flowers.

This parade on the Dia de Las Flores is the first act in which ritual roles are recognized, in this case the Mayordoma. The hermandad comes down from the Era de la Cuesta in double file. The people in each file hold branches in such a way as to make an arch. Then the Mayordoma walks between two girls designated as *Diputadas*. These three are just behind the tamborilero and the leaders of the two lines who play the tamborines. Rockets are fired nonstop. When the Llano reaches their cross and end their parade, the Fuente enters town from the other side. Until quite recently both brotherhoods came into town simultaneously, but cases of pushing and shoving and hair-pulling, as well as firing of rockets into the crowd, forced the civil authorities to put them on a rigid time schedule.

After the parades each hermandad holds a traditional dance. These take place in rented halls where the secular festivities are held. Traditional dances have the tamborilero as music maker. Non-traditional dances are those which have modern electrified bands as replacements for the old pattern of guitar, mandolin and drum bands. As the dance breaks up at about one A.M., the Night of the Pines begins.

NOCHE DE LOS PINOS

Each hermandad takes to the street behind its tamborilero and spends the night singing through the town. Partisan feeling is running high. Along with rockets, the night is punctuated with cries of "Viva la calle de la Fuente!" and "Viva el Llano!" Although every active member is supposed to stay up, by three o'clock, most have gone to bed. When most people have slipped off, the core of stalwart boys continues to go about town. By about three-thirty, when only a dozen or so remain on the streets, an odd bit of pragmatism creeps through. One of the tamborileros goes off to nap and the boys from both crosses go around together. At five they begin to bang on the shuttered windows of those who didn't stay up. Abruptly the group splits back into two parties and they each go about waking their members.

At this point the *Noche de los Pínos* has its climax. Each group goes out in the predawn darkness to the pine groves on their side of town. They cut down four pine trees, each about twenty feet high. These pine trees, like the chubarba, are indispensible ritual elements of the Cross ceremony. Just at daybreak the groups come into town carrying the trees. They are still singing fandangos of the cross, many of which are love songs. But on the morning of the pines, some are closer to the central feeling of the moment than others.

El fandago es mi alegría
el cante que llegue al cielo
que quita las penas mias
un fandango de la Fuente.
(Fandango de la Cruz - La Fuente)

The fandango is my
happiness,
the song that reaches to
Heaven,
that dispels my sorrows,
a fandango from the Fuente.

*   *

La luna va caminando
por la vere'a del cielo
en cuando en cuando se para
por ver el color de tu pelo
y los ojos de tu cara.

The moon goes journeying
on the path of the sky,
from time to time it stops
to see the color of your hair
and your eyes.

These are popular fandangos sung throughout the night; but the song that is sung most, as the trees are actually brought into the plaza of the cross, is closest to the spirit of that moment.

Toda la noche me llevo
atravesando pinares
por darle los Buenos Dias
al Divino Sol que sale.

All night I've spent
crossing through pine
groves
to say good morning
to the divine sun that
rises.

This is the moment at which the cross itself is fully decorated. The four pine trees, undecorated, are erected at the four corners of the cross. The chubarba arch is attached to the pillar to frame the cross. Paintings of Christ on the cross and tapestries are hung on the pillar itself, with more paper flowers and chubarba. Potted lilies and other real flowers are placed on the ground around the cross, within the pine tree boundaries. A red carpet is laid, leading to the front of the cross. A white silk scarf is draped over the cross itself, symbolic of a shroud.

SUNDAY OF THE CROSS

By eight A.M. the crosses are decorated and everyone goes home to dress for the ritual of the Day of the Cross. With the crosses adorned, some of the important stylistic differences between the two traditions of the brotherhoods are apparent. The Fuente uses more plastic flowers than paper ones. Their crowning achievement is a cross of fluorescent lights which they mount in front of the ornamental iron cross itself, completely obscuring it. To one group these are *"cosas de lujo y de mérito"* ("things of luxury and merit"); to the other they are *"tonterías"* ("stupidities"), which show the laziness and lack of pride of the Fuente. Differences are the grounds for contention which each group seizes upon to enhance its own image at the expense of the other.

This is the day of the Romerías, the parades called Romeros which are the major ritual on the Crosses festival. The ritual is called a romería, "pilgrimage," because the parades go outside the town and into the countryside, symbolically, that is, since they go no farther than the Era de la Cuesta. Each parade is the mirror image of the other, and most of the songs are the same with only minor variations. Both the ritual's meaning and geography of the town fix the parade route. One group follows it clockwise; the other counter clockwise. Figure 3–1 simplifies this description.

Starting at its own cross, each group takes a short loop which is the "search for the Mayordoma." Then it proceeds from the cross to the Era de la Cuesta where the Mayordomo waits. After reentering town, the group goes to the opposition's cross. Before returning to the home cross, each brotherhood visits the church and the ayuntamiento. Although the parades have always taken turns, first one hermandad's and then the other's, in the past one group often jumped the gun and thus their paths would cross. Civil authority has settled the question with its time table. First the Romero of the Fuente at midmorning; then the official mass for the Day of the Cross with its own nonsectarian procession; then the secular festivity of the Mayordomos of the Fuente, a lavish refresco; then in the afternoon, the Romero of the Llano; the secular contribution of the Llano mayordomos is held at midnight in the Llano, a spectacular fireworks display. In the past, the late afternoon used to be left open for a bull fight, but impresarios now consider the weather not good enough for

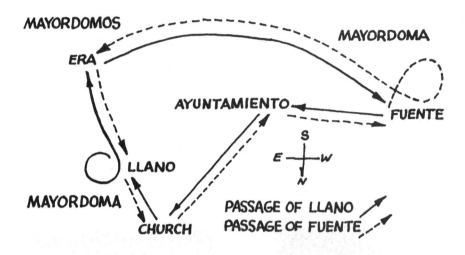

FIGURE 3-1   Schematic representation of the Romería Route And its Main Stages. One possible point of confusion is the use of Almonaster "perspective." When conceptualizing the town, North is down, South is up, East is left and West is right in any graphic representation.

a worthwhile crowd at this early date in the year, and the fight is seldom held. Finally both groups have large dances with modern rock-and-roll bands, which go until three or four in the morning.

Romero de La Cruz

Each Romero goes through the same major stages. First, all of the girls dressed in their serrana costumes gather at the cross with their tambourines and the tamborilero. There are constant rocket explosions, and a great crowd of members of the hermandad gather around them. The Mayordomo and his two Diputados, the only male roles in the Romero, and the Mayordoma and her two Diputadas are not present. When the crowd has built to a respectable size, the serranas set out in double file, singing and following the tamborilero, to "look for the Mayordoma." As they go they sing a number of coplas describing the reason for the veneration of the cross, some of which are reproduced on p. 71. They also sing coplas specifically composed for this part of the ritual notably:

Donde está la Mayordoma,	Where is the Mayordoma,
donde está que no la veo?	where is she that I don't
Andaremos un pasito,	see her?
más adelante la veremos.	We will walk a bit,
(Copla del Romero)	farther ahead we will see
	her.

*

Ya vienen las golondrinas,	Now come the swallows,
con la pechugita blanca,	with their little white
anunciando que María	breasts,
fue concebida sin mancha.	announcing that Mary
(Copla del Romero)	was conceived without sin.

*

Donde está la Mayordoma	Where is the Mayordoma
de la Santa Cruz del Llano?	of the sainted Cross of the
Dios le dé mucha salud	Llano?
para serle muchos años.	God give her health
(Copla del Romero - el Llano)	to be it [mayordoma] for
	many years.

They find the Mayordoma and her Diputadas in the doorway of her house. The Mayordoma carries the most important ritual element, the Bandera, a banner embroidered in gold and silver thread on a white background. It represents the cross itself and is the highest ritual offering. After a serenade by the serranas, the Mayordoma, flanked by her Diputadas, joins the parade.

The next stage in the Romero is two-fold, seeking the Mayordomo and going into the *campo* to pick the herb *romero*, "rosemary," the symbol of the pilgrim and the second highest offering. Both of these are accomplished by parading out to the Era de la Cuesta where the Mayordomo is waiting on horseback. (The romero is already picked and being carried by those who will need it during the ritual.) The parade marches out of town with singing, cries of "viva la Cruz del Llano" or "de la Fuente." The rockets are constant and neither the people nor the waiting horses are flinching at the explosions any more. As they go, the two themes of picking romero and finding the Mayordomo are reiterated in the coplas:

Vamos por el romerito,	We go for the romero,
vamos en gracia de Dios,	we go in the grace of God,

que está florido y hermoso
para la Cuz del Señor.

            *

Mayordomo de la Cruz?
allí lo tienes parado
en la Era de la Cuesta,
montado en su caballo.
(Coplas del Romero)

that it is flowered and
beautiful
for the Cross of our Lord.

            *

Mayordomo of the Cross?
there you have him stopped
on the Era de la Cuesta,
mounted on his horse.

As the Mayordomo waits on his horse, the parade approaches the Era de la Cuesta. It is really less of a parade than a great cheering and singing mass with a colorful center. Everyone who can take the trip follows the Romero closely. The hermandad supplies its own audience wherever it goes. The serranas are hemmed in on all sides by the rest of the hermandad in suits and dresses. On the Era an important transfer takes place, and the symbolism of the Mayordomo's role is made more apparent. Again it is the songs of the Cross which most clearly convey the religious symbolism. First the transfer of the bandera from the Mayordoma to the Mayordomo:

Mayordomo de la Cruz
acercate a la Bandera
porque ya viene cansada
la pobre de tu compañera.
(Copla del Romero)

Mayordomo of the Cross
come close to the Banner
because your poor companion
arrives tired.

The transfer is made amid cries of "Viva La Mayordoma," "Viva el Mayordomo" and "Viva La Cruz . . . " As they parade back into town to the next stage at the opposite cross, they are lead by the Mayordomo, flanked by his Diputados, and carrying the Banner. As they enter town a new copla is aired:

Dicen que en Jerusalén
un gran capitán ha entrado
con una Cruz en los hombros,
tres veces arrodillado.

They say that in Jerusalem
a great captain has entered
with a cross on his shoulders,
three times on his knees.

The next stage, the courtesy visit to the opposition's cross, is a concrete meeting of the religious values and motives of the brotherhoods with the secular process which the Almuñenses sum up in the phrase, "to be very partisan." Up to this point the competition between hermandades has been in terms of doing the same things and comparing performances. Now that the parade must make its courtesy call on the opposition cross, this competition changes to more open rivalry on the part of the visiting hermandad. There is important ritual to be carried out at the foot of the opposition's cross, but though this may be carried out with real reverence, the paraders cannot resist the opportunity for some gentle teasing of the opposition on their own home ground.

The ritual at the opposition's cross involves circling the cross three times during which the Mayordomos present bundles of romero as tokens of respect and recognition, all the while singing the most worshipful of coplas. As the rockets explode and the crowd, made up of many from the hermandad of the opposition, shout their "vivas" to the cross, the marchers can remain pious no longer. On their way out of the plaza, they air their newest compositions. These are almost always aimed at some specific individual in the opposition parade and at some specific known defect or idiosyncracy. The Fuente which parades in the Llano in the morning always gets the first shot in. They always seem able to compose the most telling coplas:

Que es aquello que relumbra en la Era de la Cuesta? Las pestañas de Fernanda qué no las tiene bien puesta. (Copla del Romero—la Fuente)	What is that which shines brightly on the Era de la Cuesta? Fernanda's eyelashes which she doesn't have on right.

In this case the butt of the copla was the Mayordoma of the Llano. Even members of the Llano in the audience had to laugh. The paraders keep their expressions of rivalry on this safe personal level, but in the audience there may be an escalation of rivalry to the point of bickering and real annoyance if the cooler heads fail to be careful and to watch out for less controlled hermanos.

After this offering and the veneration of the opposition cross, there are two important stages before the final veneration of the cross of the hermandad. One is the recognition of secular authority as the parade passes in front of the ayuntamiento. The other is the entrance into the church to venerate the cross inside. At each stage gifts of romero are made signifying respect, courtesy and devotion. The stop in church seems a veneration of the divinity within the church rather than of the church as religious authority.

There is in fact a history of friction between the town and the church over this ceremony. The people feel that this stage is the most repugnant to the church heirarchy because it excludes the priest and includes the playing of the tamborilero and the singing of the serranas. The parades enter by the Great Door and worship at the foot of a special *paso* of the cross which is used in the church's own Day of the Cross procession. Here the songs are in praise and reverence to the Cross and the Passion. An occasional petition for health to all the hermanos is made, but joy in following the Mayordoma in venerating the Cross seems to predominate.

Las serranas de la Fuente	The serranas of the Fuente
estan todas muy contentas	are all very glad
pues para ofrecer el romero	as to offer the romero
en la Santa Iglesia entran.	they enter the sainted
(Copla del Romero—la Fuente)	Church.

After the offering of the romero, the Mayordoma leads the parade out through the Great Door to where the Mayordomo waits on his horse with the bandera. This use of the Great Door is indicative of the ritual "charge" with which the parade is endowed; a very holy procession venerating the presence of a very holy symbol.

Because of the geography of the town each parade must pass through the central plaza twice during the romería, but the route is carefully planned so that they pass in front of the ayuntamiento only once. As the parade passes the open doorway of the ayuntamiento, the alcalde, or one of his representatives, accepts the offerings of the hermandad. First the Mayordomo and then the Mayordoma present him with branches of romero. It is symbolic recognition of the secular authority of the town. Along with the romero goes a serenade of coplas to the alcalde, thanking him specifically for allowing the ceremony.

Bendito sea el alcalde	Blessed by the alcalde
que la licencia nos dió	who gave us permission
para ir por el romero	to go for the romero
después de Misa Mayor	after High Mass.
*	*
Bendito sea el alcalde	Blessed be the alcalde
que a la puerta ha asomado	who has leaned out the door
a recibir el romero	to receive the romero

de la Santa Cruz del Llano.   of the Santa Cruz del Llano.
(Coplas del Romero—el Llano)

The alcalde, on the step of the ayuntamiento, is flanked by two of his lieutenant alcaldes or other members of the town council. Flanking the door are the night watchman and the "bailiff" (*alguacil*), in their best municipal uniforms as guards. In practice it is not the actual alcalde himself who accepts the homage of the crosses. The present alcalde is partisan of one hermandad. Rather than let this disrupt him or the smooth functioning of his office, he delegates two sets of representatives from the council, one to meet the Llano and one for the Fuente. They are either members of the hermandad they greet or truly neutral people.

After the church and the ayuntamiento are visited, the hermandad returns to their own cross to end the ceremony. This is one of the most important points of the entire ceremony and the plaza is jammed. Every member who is not following the parade is waiting here. Members of the other cross are here to see the event. Spectators from the aldeas and other parts of Andalucía all mill about. The little bars set up just for the festival do a crashing business.

As the hermandad enters the plaza, the cheers and the rockets drown out the singing. Just enough room is left in the plaza to let the parade come to the foot of the cross. The parade led by the Mayordomo circles the cross three times. Then the Mayordomo, usually with a good deal of help, coaxes his horse up to the front of the cross where he presents a branch of romero. Then he moves back and the Mayordoma, flanked by the diputadas and the rest of the serranas, faces the cross.

Acercate Mayordoma   Go close Mayordoma
y pon romero en la Cruz   and put romero on the Cross
que en ella crucificaron   for on it was crucified
a nuestro padre Jesús.   our father Jesus.
(Copla del Romero)

The Mayordoma, to the singing of this copla, moves up to the cross and offers a branch of romero. As she returns, the serranas who separate her from the Mayordomo move aside and the Mayordomo gives the Bandera back to the Mayordoma. This is the most important moment. Again facing the cross they sing:

Que bonita esta la Cruz
que parece una paloma.
Con orgullo y devoción
se acerca the Mayordoma.
(Copla del Romero)

The cross is so beautiful
that it resembles a dove.
With pride and devotion
the Mayordoma goes to it.

The Mayordoma goes forward again and places the Bandera against the pillar of the cross. She kneels in front of the cross and everyone follows. There is a crescendo of "Vivas" for the Mayordoma, the Mayordomo, the Cross and the Hermandad. The last act of the parade is to escort the Mayordoma back to her house.

Angeles venir, venir
con laureles en la mano
a coronar a la Cruz
que nosotros ya nos vamos.
(Copla del Romero)

Angels come, come
with laurels in hand
to crown the cross
because we are leaving now.

Moments after the departure of the parade, everyone is back around the base of the cross, joined by the rest of the hermandad. They sing fandangos of the Cross to tamborines and the drum and flute of the tamborilero. Of the many secular fandangos, songs of lost and ill-favored loves are the most common. Two fandangos are very popular, and the crowd of hermanos may repeat them several times. Their lyrics come very close to expressing the fundamental meaning of the Crosses festival:

Almonaster la Real,
hermosa fiesta de Mayo,
viva las mozas serranas
de la Santa Cruz del
Llano.

Almonaster la Real,
beautiful festival of May,
hurray for the mountain girls
of the Santa Cruz del Llano.

*

*

Camino de Cortegana,
vamos todos admirados
que la mejor Cruz ha sido
la que han vesti'o en el
Llano.
(Fandangos de la Santa Cruz del Llano)

On the way to Cortegana
we are all admired
for the best cross has been
that which they adorned in
the Llano

The "Camino de Cortegana," the next big town and término to the west, starts at the Fuente. The Llano, at least, thinks that they have outdone the Fuente.

Sunday is a very long day. The two parades which make up the romerías of the two crosses are only part of the activities. The Mass at mid-day features a procession complete with paso of the cross. The procession carries the paso to both of the decorated crosses. Many of the serranas from the Fuente are still in costume. The rest of the town is in their best clothes. The two tamborileros play for the procession which is strictly non-partisan. Afterwards the Mayordomos of the Fuente put on a great refresco for their hermanos. In the Llano, the parade has not yet taken place, but the plaza is full. A small bar is open there, just for the festival, and tables and folding chairs are set up. There is much drinking and general merriment.

In the evening the dances start. Each hermandad has hired a rock-and-roll band and a dance hall for the three nights of the festival. Each dance has a bar and a sitting area. The bands are fully electrified, and the older women have to shout to hear one another. "We had fifteen more serranas in our Romero than they had for the Fuente." The men discuss the bull fights or soccer scores across tables cluttered with glasses and bottles. The older children dance and flirt. Single boys and some men pass from one dance to the other. At midnight the dancers pause, and everyone goes to the Llano where the hermandad puts on an exciting fireworks display. And then everyone returns to the dances. The last bar does not close until daybreak.

Sunday's festivities do not represent a cathartic venting of the partisanness which Las Flores and the rituals have labored to create. Neither brotherhood has really outdone the other even in its own eyes. The merit is intrinsic. It was there before the festival. Because there is simply no clear-cut way of judging "victory," the competition continues on Monday.

ROMERITO DE LOS NIÑOS

On Monday the romerías of the Llano and the Fuente are repeated in their entirety. The only difference between the parades of Sunday and Monday are the paraders themselves. The paraders on Monday are children and babies. Leading the lines and playing the tambourines are the youngest girls who marched on Sunday. On Sunday they marched at the very end of the lines; now they lead them. At the end of Monday's parades are tiny toddlers. In the costume of serranas, they are helped along by their mothers or older girls. Instead of a young man for Mayordomo, there is a nine or ten year-old boy. He rides a donkey. The trip to the Era de la Cuesta, fraught with stony trails and hills, is shortened to a march to the bridge at the edge of town, which leads to the trail to the Era. The church is closed to the children's parade. Otherwise the ritual is the same. The church bells, the rockets, the tamborilero, the singing, the audience all are the same. Needless to say, Monday is not a work day except for the bartenders, waiters and musicians.

END OF THE FESTIVAL

Just after dinner on Monday evening, while the band members are still on their dinner break, the hermandades gather at their crosses. They sing all the songs of the Cross and then parade around their half of the town. Although Sunday is the parade of the *Mozas* (the "young girls") and on Monday the privilege falls to the niñas (little girls), Monday evening is for everyone, old and young, married and single. There are no costumes, but rockets are fired by the hundreds. At the end, at the base of the cross, the Mayordomos for the coming year are named. The Bandera is given to the new Mayordoma by the old. The old Mayordoma will be one of the Diputadas for the girl who is named tonight. This year's Mayordomo will be a Diputado next year.

The dances begin again, and for a second time, they go through the night. At the bar, the adults drink incredible quantities of cognac, sherry, wine, aguardiente, and beer. This is one of the few times during the year when drunkenness is permissible, when the strictures of formalidad are loosened. Contingents come to the dances from the aldeas and other términos of the area. The entrance fees and the profits from the bar are counted on to help the hermandad bear the expense.

On Tuesday, the hermandades are still quite separate. In the afternoon each goes on a gira to their picnic site. The hermandad supplies all the wine and tapas, the musicians from the bands, and the tamborileros provide the music for dancing. At nightfall each hermandad makes the last procession of the year as it marches into town. The last dance of the festival begins.

Wednesday everyone sleeps late, and in the late afternoon preparations for the third and final festival in the cycle begin.

SANTA EULALIA: UNITY OF ALMONASTER

The overall effect of the Crosses festival is the creation of two equal, highly self-conscious, groups through the liberation and channeling of emotional energy. From an unstated cultural unity at Easter time, two very conscious social groups have emerged. These are "first level" groups because they represent a first stage of integration within the community. A "second level" of integration, a unified community, has yet to emerge. The *Romería of Santa Eulalia* is the ritual which reifies this social unity, at which the community emerges as a conscious social group.

The ritual of Santa Eulalia not only is one of the most important festivals for Almonaster, but also is the most important of a number of events within the entire multicommunity. In this chapter, Santa Eulalia is considered only as a segment of the important ritual cycle of the community of Almonaster. The wider applications of this key ritual must wait until the next chapter.

The organization of the festival of Santa Eulalia revolves around a single sodality. The *Hermandad de Santa Eulalia de Mérida* is the name of the organization, but in the context of the actual presentation of the rite, it is simply called the *Hermandad*. The site of the performance is called Santa Eulalia as is the saint herself. The hermandad is directed by a Directiva of several individuals belonging to rich families. Each of these individuals is either the head of a wealthy family or in the generation which controls it. The members of the *directiva* are all men, but the power of certain older, rich women is commonly acknowledged; thus they also participate in administrative activities. There is an *Hermano Mayor* who is the chief administrator, but decisions are made by the Directiva as a group. Many of the individuals on the Directiva have been Mayordomos of the ritual in the past, but this is not a prerequisite. As members of the Directiva, they are not elected and have no fixed period of tenure.

Each year the members of the Directiva announce the names of the Mayordomos for the coming year. These posts, Mayordomo and Mayordoma, are the most public and the most expensive. Besides leading the ritual, they are responsible for funding a great deal of it. In addition, most Mayordomos contribute substantially to the physical plant at Santa Eulalia during their tenure. This may be in terms of repairs or actual new construction. The Mayordomos are extremely important, but they are not indispensible. In the absence of a Mayordomo, the festival can and does go on, although it won't be as "good" or as "happy."

Mayordomos are usually from the rich families, but this is not a hard and fast rule because some have been poorer members of the hermandad.

The actual membership of the hermandad is comparatively small with only about 200 paying members. However, this is not an accurate measure of the number of devotees which Santa Eulalia commands. Membership is not a prerequisite for participation in the major ritual of Santa Eulalia. Membership, rather then being a measure of devotion or interest, seems to be a function of the amount of free cash available to an individual. Although the dues themselves are limited to what a person feels he or she can pay, they can be a burden on a small income. Nevertheless, 200 is an accurate sample of the community, with members from every segment of society. Many of the most devout followers of the saint are not members. This is particularly true of those from other communities within the multicommunity and among the poorer people in town. What is important is participation, the commitment to the saint and her festival.

Participation in the festival of Santa Eulalia is of two types. Active participants are those who go to the rural ermita, some twelve to fifteen miles into the campo, for the two days of ritual. Vicarious participants are those who would go if they could. This second group is the majority. For economic, health or mourning reasons many people are unable to go. Most of them have gone at one time or another in the past, and they hope to go again. In terms of the basic function of the reification of the unity of the social group, both kinds of participation are equally valid and important.

The veneration of Santa Eulalia takes place in three distinct divisions. Immediately following the final rite of the Crosses, the first phase begins. This is nine days of minor ritual, performed nightly. This attracts the actual recorded membership. Following this phase is the second major ritual, the Romería. Coming nine days after the Crosses, this major ritual is always on the third weekend in May. The third ritual is again minor, at least from the point of view of Santa Eulalia's social unity functions. This is the celebration of Santa Eulalia's "day" (December 10) as it appears in the Roman Catholic calender.[3] The celebration is a mass and refresco for the hermanos. This analysis will ignore the third phase completely because it is peripheral to the three-festival cycle.

Like the Crosses of May, the "meaning" of Santa Eulalia is best seen in the folk literature associated with her. Again this is in the form of a vast repertoire of songs. The song style involved here is the fandango. The Fandangos de Santa Eulalia are a recognized genre not only within the area, but also in the rest of Spain as well, where they are sometimes known as *Fandangos de Almonaster*; a mistake that Almuñenses find a bit offensive.

Unlike the fandangos of the Cross, which are also fandangos of Almonaster, the Fandango of Santa Eulalia is sung all year long, except for the time between Easter and the festival of Santa Eulalia when the fandango of the Cross reigns. By tradition these two bodies of fandangos are not sung together. Those of the Cross are only sung during the specific period of the year. This distinction between the fandangos, supports the point made earlier that the "first level" groups created by the Crosses are a temporary state while the "second level" group which emerges from Santa Eulalia is the rule during the rest of the year.

The importance of the fandangos to the rest of the ritual of Santa Eulalia is amply illustrated by the following popular fandango:

Almonaster fué tu cuna	Almonaster was your cradle,
fandango santoolallero,	fandango of Santa Eulalia,
Almonaster te dió fama,	Almonaster gave you fame.
no quiero tono alosnero	I don't like the Alosno style
porqué no me llega alma.	because it doesn't reach
(Fandango de Santa Eulalia)	the soul.

This fandango contains a number of significant allusions. It emphasizes that all Fandangos of Santa Eulalia are local creations arising out of devotion to the saint, and that each one touches the soul of the singer or hearer. The reference to the Alosno style of singing these fandangos is more subtle because it is the style in which these fandangos have been popularized over the rest of Spain. Alosno is a pueblo of Southern Huelva, famous for its professional singers. When these professionals interpret fandangos from other places, they give them a distinctive Alosno flavor. When the professionals change their style of the fandangos, the people of Almonaster feel that part of the message changes also. Although many of the fandangos have quite secular themes, there is a feeling of the sanctity of all of them. Whatever the topic, "it comes from the soul." There is a "truth" to all fandangos.

Two of the most popular fandangos, whose "truth" is indisputable, demonstrate two of the most central considerations of the ritual.

La Virgen de Santa Eulalia,	The Virgin of Santa Eulalia,
la que más altares tiene;	the (Virgin) who has the
no hay uno en Almonaster	most altars;
que en su pecho no la lleve.	there is no one in

(Fandango de Santa Eulalia)   Almonaster
                                               who doesn't carry her in
                                               his breast.

                    *   *

Cuando de lejos deviso   When from a distance I
el castillo de mi pueblo   espy
un relincho da mi jaca   the castle of my town
y galopa más que el viento;   my pony gives a whinny
que la querencia la mata.   and gallops faster than
(Fandango de Santa Eulalia)   the wind;
                                               that the love of home
                                               would kill her.

Devotion to the saint is universal within the community. That same profound emotion is associated with the community itself. The symbol of
Almonaster in this case is the tower of the castle, the first feature that
one can see as he approaches through the mountain valleys. It is also a
neutral symbol in terms of the Crosses. (A more detailed analysis of the
fandangos is found in Appendix 2.)

The neutrality of Santa Eulalia, with respect to the Crosses, is also
evident in the physical setting of the ermita. Although the hermandad
owns some of the outbuildings at Santa Eulalia, the ground belongs to
the Ayuntamiento and thus the ground is part of the public lands of the
término. Certainly the geographic isolation of Santa Eulalia, out in the
campo and off the road, lends itself to her position as a symbol of unity.
She is quite literally set apart from the partisan concerns of the Crosses
or of everyday life.

Another characteristic of the setting is important. Santa Eulalia is the
ruins of a Roman mining town. The ermita itself is the only visible
vestige of those times. The base and part of the back wall of the ermita
are part of a small Roman temple and along the paths and between the
tree roots, the vestiges of ancient house foundations remain. Each year
when the hermandad or some adjoining land owner sends men in to work
on the dirt road, they unearth some new Roman curiosity. Admittedly,
there is an age-old discussion among the common people as to whether it
is a Roman or Moorish town, but the more educated townspeople are con-
vinced of Santa Eulalia's Roman origin, in spite of countless tales of
Moorish princesses and treasures, because of the occasional Roman in-
scriptions. Regardless of the origin, all agree that it was a city preceding
the existence of Almonaster. What better place for the most sacred of

symbols: a Spanish girl martyred by Romans. As the story is told in Almonaster, Eulalia was transported after her martyrdom from the great city of Mérida, to the north of Almonaster, to the smaller city, now in ruins, which bears her name. Like the Crosses she is an autochthonous symbol. Even though the account of the movement of her body to the mining town is only documented in the local folklore, the veneration of the saint is certainly an old custom. The existence of the Romería can be certified back to 1774 when Don Gregorio del Valle was the Mayordomo.

Although Santa Eulalia is symbol of unity for Almonaster, and therefore her veneration the concern of the whole community as well as of the hermandad, this does not preclude the existence of important role and status differences within the festival. The festival reifies a kind of organic solidarity which recognizes these role and status differences. Such differential participation and position is most apparent during the minor phases of the ritual and in the more secular of the rituals.

The Novena

The first phase of the ritual is the Novena; nine days of evening prayer for the saint, held in the church in Almonaster. This is a religious preparation for the actual Romería and veneration of the image. Before each service there is a secular celebration for the hermandad.

Wednesday, the day after the gira and last dance of the Crosses, is a normal workday. Everyone is exhausted but back on the job. The town is quiet after the noise and gaiety of the Crosses. At six-thirty the first of three calls to church is given, calling people to the novena of Santa Eulalia. The normal call to church is the ringing of the bells. For the novena of Santa Eulalia, the first call of each evening is with rockets. The rockets do not simply inform the people that the novena will start at seven-fifteen, they also indicate the opening of the Mayordomo's house to the hermanos. At the open house all members are welcome. Tapas and sherry are served. Poorer hermanos tend to be quieter, to leave sooner. Everyone may be equal in the eyes of the saint, but people don't forget the social differences as easily. The difference is not blatant; just a difference in degree rather than in kind. At the last call, the Mayordomo leads everyone in his house to the church. His symbol of authority is a silver staff. Flanking him are several of the Directiva carrying wooden staves with silver tops.

The first night seems the most important because fewer people tend to be there on the succeeding nights. Only those members who are not otherwise busy come to the house and the novena. Consequently the meetings tend to be dominated by the wealthier members, who generally make up the group from which the majority of office holders is drawn.

The novena itself involves the recitation of some standard prayers in front of a surrogate image of the saint. Although the novena should be in front of the saint herself, a substitute is used because she is so far away. For the occasion a framed picture is placed in a special altar and surrounded by candles. The same arrangement is employed for the December celebration of her day. Normally her picture hangs on the left front wall of the church so that all of the community's religious Patrons are accessible to everyone during the year.

The novena is neither a festive nor a cathartic experience, and it is usually poorly attended. In contrast, the Romería, which comes at the end of the nine day novena, is the major ritual of Santa Eulalia. It functions as the cathartic and unifying ritual that ends the entire festival cycle. Since Friday is the last day of the novena, it is also the day when supplies are sent out to Santa Eulalia. Traditionally a mule train load with all the food and drink and other provisions sets out on this day. Now these supplies all go by truck, but the rest of the ritual still goes on as in the past. When the tamborilero walks through the streets playing for the cargo as it leaves town, the Romería of Santa Eulalia has truly begun.[4]

The Romería

The Romería, which takes place on Saturday, is a pilgrimage out to Santa Eulalia. Traditionally it is done on horse and mule back. Nowadays many people go in cars and trucks organized by the hermandad, but there still are some who go in the old style; mostly young people. In the Romería at least half of all the animals and saddlery used is borrowed from one or two of the richest men. Friday is the time when people rush around making last minute preparations, including arrangements for picking up the borrowed equipment. In the evening the tamborilero again goes through the streets playing. This time he may collect a following of singers and together they go about. Eventually they will end up serenading the Mayordomo, who will come to the door with wine, aguardiente, and tobacco.

At seven-thirty on Saturday morning rockets explode and the tamborilero starts through the streets. People attend to the saddling of horses and mules. The girls and women all dress in the ruffled dresses made famous by Flamenco singers and dancers. Although this costume is not traditional in the sierra, it has become the standard festival outfit of all of Andalucía. Rich men wear handsome riding outfits; poorer men and boys simply wear clean clothes. The mules have great cushion-like pack saddles, the horses have a special pad attached behind the saddle. Behind each horseman or mule rider, sits *una gitana*, a "gypsy girl," who grips him tightly around the waist as she rides side-saddle. By ten o'clock there are mounted couples waiting in the plaza next to the church and on side streets, eager to begin the romería. When the Mayordomos seem to be ready, all of the couples ride down the cobblestone streets to their house. The Mayordomos are on horseback along with several of the Directiva. Each bears the staff of his office. If not enough of the Directiva can be found willing to ride in the fairly treacherous parade, their staffs are given to some of the horsemen to carry. Led by the Mayordomos all of the couples begin a circuit through town. The streets are lined with spectators who cheer for everyone, rockets explode continuously, the tamborilero plays his drum and flute. Nervous horses and mules start at every sudden and loud noise, their hooves slip and clatter along the steep stone streets.

After a turn or two, the Mayordomos and Directiva drop out and the couples who will actually make the trip make one last turn of the town. It is a short one, just far enough to pass the door of the casino. At the casino a free glass of sherry is available for each of the romeros, the pilgrims. This is only the first of many drinks as the following fandango indicates:

De la uva sale el vino
Viva el vino y la alegría!
aquel que vino no beba
que se vaya, que se vaya
lejos de la Romería.
(Fandango de Santa Eulalia
by Francisco Montero
Escalera)

From the grape comes the
wine
Hurray for wine and
  happiness!
He that doesn't drink wine
should go, he should go
far from the Romería.

As they ride out on the road to Santa Eulalia singing fandangos, the sun shines brightly. The temperature is in the high eighties. Just outside of town they stop and a bottle of sherry is handed around, for the singing and the dust and the heat make throats dry. Among the romeros is a man hired by the hermandad. He rides a mule with great saddle bags full of

liter bottles of sherry and containers of tapas, all for the trip to Santa
Eulalia.

Most of the route to Santa Eulalia is through the countryside. At a few
points the path passes through an aldea or large farm. The people are all
out to see the romeros, who come in singing. There is much cheering for
the saint, and the group stops in front of the local bar and someone buys
a liter of red or white wine. The taverner hands the bottle up to the
mounted pilgrims and it is passed around. To a chorus of "Viva Santa
Eulalia" the taverner usually gives a second round on the house. The
riders prepare for these entries by bunching together and all singing the
same song as they enter.

No hay cielo come aquel cielo,	There is no sky like that sky,
cielo azul de Santa Eulalia,	blue sky of Santa Eulalia,
ni rio como el Odiel	nor a river like the Odiel
donde me lavé la cara	where I washed my face
en un bello amanecer.	in a beautiful downing.
(Fandango de Santa Eulalia)	

The song alludes to the beauty of Santa Eulalia and a custom made
famous in this ritual. After a whole night of very secular merriment, the
people all go down to the stream which flows near the ermita to wash
their faces. The happy thought expressed in the gay song goes straight to
the people of the little towns. "What happiness, what splendor." Whatever jealousy the idea may evoke in the aldea stay-at-homes is not expressed; instead these bystanders call for a particular song or simply
wish everyone safe journey. By now the pilgrims are feeling the effect of
much too much sherry, in the heat, and on a fairly empty stomach. But
no one is ill or even uncomfortable; "Santa Eulalia would not let it
happen."

At mid-point in the road from Almonaster to Santa Eulalia is a place
called Los Arenales. It is a rural farm. There is a large house and acres of
green grass under the shade of the encina trees. It is also the place where
the trail crosses the paved road. Those who come to Santa Eulalia by car
or truck stop here at Los Arenales. The shuttle of trucks and cars arranged by the Hermano Mayor drop their loads here and return to town
for more. Those who travel by truck or car arrive soon after the romeros
leave the town; so they while away the hours before the riders arrive by

dancing, singing, drinking and eating. There are a few regulars who always bring instruments and all of the tamborileros are present. Under the trees are a swirling mass of people, groups cluster around a guitar or mandolin or tamborilero. They dance and sing sevillanas. A few even dance to the fandangos, although this is something of a lost art. The arrival of the romeros heightens the gaiety. After the romeros have "rested" for about an hour of singing and dancing and drinking, the Romería continues.

The road from Los Arenales to Santa Eulalia is a winding gravel track, recently made passable to trucks by the hermandad. The cars and trucks begin to leave and the romeros, again on their horses and mules, hurry on too.

Dale a la jaca que ande que llegue pronto a la ermita, en la que tengo mi fé, en Santa Eulalia bendita. (Fandango de Santa Eulalia)	Give it to the pony! so she'll move along, so she'll arrive quickly at the hermitage, in which I have my faith, in blessed Santa Eulalia.

They want to reach Santa Eulalia quickly so the stops for wine are shorter and less frequent.

The cars and trucks reach Santa Eulalia first. It is an area of rolling hills. The hills are covered with low dense brush. This is a part of the término where they say one can still meet an occasional wolf. The wide valleys are rolling too, but they are typical pasture lands, close cropped grass and encina trees. Near where one of these valleys meets the course of the Odiel, one of the two major rivers of southwestern Spain, is the site of Santa Eulalia.

When the cars arrive, already many people are there. The concessionaires come a day or two early to construct taverns of poles and canvas or leaves. Under the arcade along the ermita itself are other concessions. Santa Eulalia would not be the same if Guerrero didn't sell wine and liquor at the side of the ermita. In the *"casa de la hermandad,"* a high ceilinged old building opposite the ermita, people who have been hired by the hermandad to fetch water and cook soup and make coffee receive the pilgrims. The house has only two rooms, a large front room where dancing can go on in the rain or in the cold of night, and a large kitchen. In the kitchen a fireplace large enough to roast a cow attests to the recently ended practice of the hermandad giving large meals to everyone who came. Now all that is left is the soup, which is the best way to sober up just enough to keep going. Beside the *casa* of the Hermandad are smaller windowless apartments. These are owned by certain of the rich families. While most people must pass the night under the encinas, if they sleep at all, the rich families have their cots and pillows.

The road into Santa Eulalia comes abruptly over a hill. At the top of this rise the romeros wait. To the left, along the ridge, is a large undecorated bull ring, below and to the right are the backs of the *casas de la hermandad* and of the rich people, beyond them is the ermita itself. When all of the girls have straightened their skirts and the Mayordomos have come out, the romeros ride down to the ermita. This is the *entrada,* entrance, of the romeros and an important piece of the ritual because it represents the official arrival of the hermandad. It is the beginning of the veneration of Santa Eulalia. They ride down and circle the ermita three times, singing fandangos. This is the hermandad's greeting to Santa Eulalia. Later a smaller group of riders will arrive in the same fashion from the nearby aldea of Patrás, but the first party is the official entry. Everyone is laughing and singing and most are already drunk; a very secular greeting. As the group circles the ermita, one girl was heard to say, "This is when it is best, now the whole town is united again." This statement comes from a person who has been a Mayordoma of the Cross, and all of whose brothers have been Mayordomos of the same cross. The unity that Santa Eulalia brings is not an unconscious one.

The entrada takes place at about three or three-thirty on Saturday afternoon. It is followed by an hour or more of singing and dancing and especially eating and more drinking. Santa Eulalia is another special time during the year when the formalidad stricture against overdrinking is suspended; thus people wander all over the area picnicing and partying. At four or four-thirty the most important of the secular rituals takes place. If the whole experience with its singing, riding, staying up all night and massive drinking may be said to be physically cathartic, to create a kind of solidarity simply through common experience, then the ritual which follows is the specific part of the festival which crystalizes the secular aspect of Santa Eulalia. This is the ritual of the bullfight.

The hermandad buys one fighting bull for the occasion and because of the laws of Spain, they also hire a licensed bullfighter, a has-been to be sure. At six o'clock the Hermano Mayor spreads a blanket near the bull-ring and, with a few other men, begins to sell tickets to the fight. The ring fills slowly. Finally all of the people are perched on the high stone ring. The women in their flamenco outfits brighten the gray and crumbling walls. The professional bullfighter goes to the center of the ring, hoping to make a heroic first confrontation with the bull. As the bull charges into the ring, there is an involuntary gasp from the crowd at the awesome force of a fighting bull. Then the ring is suddenly swarming with most of the men and boys. They surround the bull fighter, relieve him of his cape and sword, and help him out of the ring. The crowd begins to fight the bull.

Confronted by so many inebriated persons, the bull has no trouble mauling many. People seem to be falling down everywhere at once. Don José, a rich and important man, is tossed by the bull; this is the first time he has been bested by a bull at Santa Eulalia in forty-five years. In their haste to get out of the charging bull's path, two young boys trip and fall against the base of the wall. The bull's horns miss them, but they dislodge over one hundred pounds of wall from the decaying arena onto the boys' backs. The taxi driver, always a good bullfighter, leads the bull away with a few deft passes. People run to uncover the boys, "of course they are unhurt. Did Don José get hurt? Santa Eulalia would not let it happen!" On occasion a rib or an arm is broken, but miraculously never a life lost. Such immunity to serious injury is not the result of skill or heroism on the part of the fighters, but clearly because of the Saint's protection.

There is a famous story in Almonaster which illustrates the power of the saint in several ways. Because of the has-been nature of the professional bullfighter, an important part of the bullfight is missing. This is the picador, the man on horseback who prepares the bull with a long lance. The picador saps some of the strength of the bull so that the bullfighter can work with him during the finale of the fight. Picadors are expensive and there never is one at Santa Eulalia. Years ago two friends who were quite drunk decided that they would add this role to the fight at Santa Eulalia. So Ricardo, the carpenter, a man perhaps five-feet-two inches in height and weighing little more than a hundred pounds, took his young friend Manuel onto his shoulders. With a short two-by-four for a lance, Manuel played picador. Each year they came out into the center of the ring and each year the bull made short work of them. They did this until Ricardo was in his late sixties, long after Manuel had grown to his six-foot, 180-pound manhood. Neither was hurt because of the power of the Saint. The people of Almonaster perceive the power of the Saint working in this illustration in two ways: the Saint's ability to protect her venerators and her power as a unifier. Ricardo was the president of the hermandad of the Llano for 16 years, and Manuel is one of the most partisan members of the Fuente.

The bullfight ends when the bull learns that there are so many targets in the ring that it is useless to try to attack any one of them. Finally he just refuses to charge at anyone. Even drunk, the crowd realizes that the bull is now at his most dangerous because it is always relatively safe to have the bull charge you, but dangerous to walk up to a standing bull. Consequently the bullfighter is left with the responsibility of killing the bull.

In the late evening the Mayordomo brings the Saint out of the ermita in the first of two processions in which everyone joins. The small and beautifully guilded image of Santa Eulalia, surrounded by sprigs of romero, is carried on her paso near the end of the procession.

The Mayordomos and Directiva with their staffs walk just in front. Before everyone goes the tamborilero and one of the several banners and standards of the saint. In the body of the procession go several other banners. The procession makes one great circle around the ermita. Light for the procession comes from hundreds of flares carried by the marchers. The tamborilero plays a special tune and the people sing a series of *Gozos*, or special couplets, in praise of the Virgin. The first nine tell of her martyrdom; the last two of the results of Eulalia's faith and sacrifice:

Entre los Santos y Santas	Among the saints
Que le Cristianidad venera,	Which Christianity
Sin segunda, eres primera	venerates,
En las maravillas tantas:	Without second, you are the
Que á los tuyos das y	First
diste	In your so many marvels:
De gracia, salud y grano.	That to yours you give and
Dános, Eulalia, la mano	gave
Y la fé que recibiste	Grace, health and grain.
	Give us, Eulalia your hand
	And the faith that you
	received.

*

De España fuiste aclamada	From Spain you were
Patrona en su Monarquía	acclaimed
Y con mucha gloria mía	Patron in your Kingdom
lo eres de esta villa	And to my great glory
amada:	You are such to this
Sí tanto favor hiciste	beloved town:
Á este tu Pueblo	Indeed so great is the favor

Cristiano.
Dános, Eulalia, la mano
Y la fé que recibiste.
(Gozos de Santa Eulalia)

you have shown
To this your Christian
people.
Give us, Eulalia, your hand
And the faith that you
received

The position of Santa Eulalia is exceptional in the life and hearts of the people. As a Patron, she overshadows the "official" Patron of Almonaster, the Virgin of Grace, whose veneration is paltry beside that of Santa Eulalia. The ritual is also exceptional because it is one of the very rare occasions when women can carry ritually charged images in a procession. In contrast, women never carry the pasos of the Semana Santa processions, nor in the *fiesta* of the patron saint of the town. This is compatible with the key festivals of the aldeas, when women also are able to carry the paso.

At midnight the dancing and drinking stop so that all can observe a dramatic display of fireworks with a special tamborilero accompaniment. Afterward the company settles in for a long night of dancing and singing. This is the perfect time for the many love song fandangos of Santa Eulalia. They are sung during the entire ritual but never so effectively.

En tu puerta siempre un
guindo,
en tu ventana un manzano;
solo pa' verte cojer
manzanitas con la mano.
(Fandango de Santa Eulalia)

At your doorway always a
cherry tree,
at your window an apple
tree;
just to see you pick
little apples with your
hand.

Those who tire of drinking and dancing and singing, sneak off to rest, often in couples.

At daybreak a band of revelers accompany the tamborilero in shaking and chiding people into wakefulness. The tamborilero plays the special *"Despierta,"* the "revale" of the romería. As the day brightens, people begin to perform one of the customs which is particular to Santa Eulalia.

Es un antiguo costumbre

It is an old custom

para todos que llegan a la función que irse y lavarse la frente, sin toalla y sin jabón. (Fandango de Santa Eulalia)	for everyone who comes to the celebration to go (to the river) and wash his face, without soap or towel.

This is just what they do. Singly and in groups, they go down to the river and wash. Many have not slept at all and the cold water does wonders.

At midmorning on Sunday there is a mass in the ermita during which the Mayordomo again brings the Saint "out to the light." The procession of the night before is repeated. As the image returns to the ermita, the crowd gathers around the paso. With the Mayordomos standing in front, the decision of the directiva is announced. Amid cheers and congratulations the Mayordomos for the coming year are named. The silver staff of office is exchanged. More than one person is moved to tears and after more congratulations, the saint is returned to the ermita and everyone retires to the casa of the hermandad. There the Mayordomo offers food and drink to everyone. Very soon the romeros are again mounted on their horses and after circling the ermita, they head back to Los Arenales.

Los Arenales is, on the return, a rest and snack break. Everyone is a bit worn, a little less ready to drink; but still very happy. The singing goes on as before. Quickly they are on the road for Almonaster again. Riding more purposefully, they are in sight of town early in the afternoon. One fandango that springs spontaneously to their lips is "when from a distance I espy the castle of my town . . ." (cf. p. 92) another goes:

Como la brasa en la lumbre Almonaster tu eres bello; nido de amor en la cumbre muy cerquita de los cielos. (Fandango de Santa Eulalia by F. Montero Escalera)	Like the live coal in the fire, Almonaster you are beautiful; nest of love at the summit, so very close to heaven.

And as they enter town, they sing to the people in the streets:

De Santa Eulalia veni'o, sin dinero y sin tobaco	From Santa Eulalia arrived, without money or tobacco,

todo lo que se dejó	all of which was left
con María Pepa y Guerrero.	with María Pepa and
(Fandango de Santa Eulalia)	Guerrero.

María Pepa and Guerrero are two well-loved taverners from Almonaster who for years have run concessions at Santa Eulalia.

The entry into Almonaster is again a parade around the town, but this time the leader is the new Mayordomo. Before the last cheer for the new Mayordomo has ceased to echo on the streets of town, most of the romeros are in bed.

Traditionally the festival ended on Monday with a gira to the Era de la Cuesta, during which the Mayordomo fed everyone in town. In recent years the Directiva made the very pragmatic decision of eliminating this part of the observance. It was one of the most expensive and, to them, the least important. Although the Mayordomo is a highly prestigious position many felt that the increasing expense of the ritual was keeping worthy Mayordomos from stepping forward and accepting the office.

CORPORATENESS, ITS REIFICATION
AND MAINTENANCE

This festival cycle can be seen as a series of ceremonies each of which completes a phase of the dual process of dissipation of tension and hostility, and the reassertion of group identity and integration. Quite clearly this is accomplished simultaneously by the conversion of the energy of dysfunctional personal tensions and hostilities toward positive group-oriented goals. The result of group identity and integration is manifest throughout the year by a high degree of social and cultural corporateness and the almost complete absence of any overt interpersonal hostility. The effectiveness of the festival cycle in dissipating social tension is further demonstrated by the fact that over a four-year period the only instances of overt hostility and tension (three in number) occurred in the months of February and March, the two months farthest from the active festival time of the cycle.

Moreover, these rituals are a refication of basic values and identities as positive goals. The values associated with "Catholicism" and formalidad are basic for individuals, but they fall short of insuring the yearlong equilibrium of the social system. Thus, the festival cycle is a graphic integration of basic personal and group level values.

The dynamics of the process are different for each festival, in keeping with the goals at each stage. In a very real way the "means" employed in each ritual become the ends. In a Catholic universe there is no difficulty in reminding people in a week-long festival that they are all basically Catholic. In terms of ritual, the high points are oriented toward the individual. The emphasis is on the interaction between the individual and the major Catholic elements of Christ, the Virgin, and the sacrament of Communion. Group activity is not in terms of a concerted communal effort so much as in the coincidence of many people participating at a particular church. Anyone can participate, anywhere.

The goal of consciousness of the group as a bounded entity, both physically and socially, is more difficult to achieve. The process employed in the Crosses is analogous to the process by which each individual first discovers his or her own "self." The experience of an "other" is a potent force in the realization of "self." Thus the Crosses channel latent hostility, to name only one basic emotional force, into ritually sanctioned directions increasing the competition between two equal segments. Competition is not necessarily the only way for two segments to become fully aware of each other. Segmental cooperation might also be employed. This is also true in the case of the Crosses, where competition is implicit in the partisanness of the members while cooperation is implied by the concept of the "good Crucero" as one who is deeply interested in the veneration of the Cross in all its guises. At least for Almuñenses, the theme of competition is by far the stronger. The first level integration which emerges from the Crosses ritual is quite impressive. The town is very graphically partitioned into two equal and highly conscious groups. Egalitarianism reigns.

But the first level of integration, maintained as it is by open competition, is a potentially dangerous force if not checked. The Crosses ritual builds the intensity of competition for each of the individuals in each of the groups, but it does not fully release the energy. Rather than negate the forces of this first level of integration, the procedure which defuses the two groups is to supersede them, giving to all a higher goal to work for as a group. The veneration of Santa Eulalia as patron, protector and dispensor of good to her people, is an exhausting group effort. It is physically cathartic. The emphasis here is on in-group cooperation, on unification.

The final reification of states at each level in the culmination of each festival is a profound experience in which each individual participates to the utmost. This participation is an almost frantic expression of physical and emotional energy. Sleeplessness and excessive alcohol obviously heighten the effect. The behavior of the participants becomes so excessive that they appear to be driven. Though exhausted, they hang on grimly enjoying the festival to their last gasp. Someone who goes to bed during the Crosses is chided for being so "weak."

The closest natural observers of this entire phenomenon are the people of the aldeas. To them much of the behavior of the rituals is plainly incomprehensible. Why the sudden partisanness that so suddenly disappears again? "The Crosses business is a stupidity. At least it is over in time for all to go as friends to Santa Eulalia." "Why should they do the Crosses that way?" Several of the aldeas venerate the cross in rituals that are carbon copies of the ones in Almonaster itself, except for the fact that none of the aldeas has two hermandades or two monumental crosses. In the aldeas the open competition is not present. The Crosses ritual functions in a different way in the aldea. Two obvious and interrelated factors probably explain the difference: first, the smaller population of the aldeas relative to Almonaster; and second, the relative unimportance of status and wealth differences in the aldeas compared to Almonaster. In the aldeas the group neither splits in two before it may be unified, nor does it have the amount of energy necessary for the creation and support of open competition. There are not enough people and too little bottled-up hostility. In the "family" atmosphere of the aldeas, people find it is harder to bear a grudge because it is easier to vent hostility at the moment, before it has become a force to be reckoned with. All of the aldeas have the same answer as reason for their lack of Cross-like partisanness, "It is very tranquil here." This is their own overstatement, as will be seen in the next chapter, but at least in the smaller context of the aldea, corporateness is not a function of *internal* competition or division of any kind. Finally the festivals not only reify group identity for those within the group, they also reaffirm that identity for local outsiders. Consequently, they outline clearly the boundaries between groups and define explicitly community limits.

NOTES

[1] For a list of the rituals in Almonaster see Appendix 3.

[2] As presented here, these song types are set in a literary form for the purpose of cursory content analysis. To do this all repetitions, etc., have been eliminated. When sung they are from five to nine lines long. The *coplas del Romero* are the longest.

For further discussion of songs and song types see Appendix 2.

³The timing of the festivals is particularly instructive in the analysis of this cycle's functions. The timing of the Romería is fully arbitrary, not being bound by the Roman Catholic
calender. This propitious timing seems to lend some credence to an analysis of the cycle as
a kind of schismogenesis (Bateson, 1958:176-177). See Chapter 5 for a fuller discussion.

⁴By almost uncanny coincidence, the relationship between the Crosses and Santa Eulalia
is mirrored in the relationship between tamborileros in Almonaster. There are three, all of
whom are at times hired to play in other parts of the province, but none of them is fully
professional. Each has his own economic pursuits in the town. The "uncanny coincidence"
is that the traditional tamborilero of the Llano is the brother of the tamborilero of the
Fuente—their father is tamborilero of Santa Eulalia!

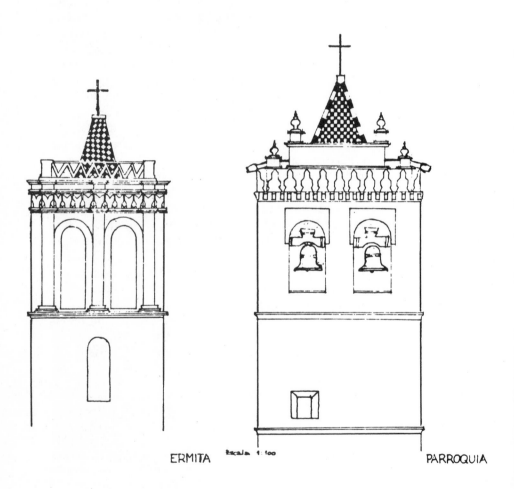

ERMITA   Escala 1:100   PARROQUIA

TORRES DE ALMONASTER
ALZADOS POR EL SUR

The paso of the Virgin leaves the Great Door of the church for an evening procession during Holy Week.

Members of eight families picnic on Easter Sunday.

At popular picnic spots, people dance and play games during the afternoon.

The Cross of the Fuente ready for the ritual. The cross itself is obscured by the fluorescent light cross which, along with plastic flowers, has been added to the traditional decorations.

The Mayordomo of the Fuente with the Bandera leading the romería into town.

Serranas and tamborilero of the Fuente escort the Mayordoma, in her distinctive hat, through the town.

A serrana of the Fuente holds the Bandera of the Brotherhood at the foot of the cross.

Romería of the Llano on its way to meet the Mayordomo on the threshing floor outside the town.

The Mayordomo of the Llano carries the Bandera at the head of the romería as it enters town.

Serranas of the Llano playing tamborines and singing as the romería reenters the town.

The romería of the Llano on the way to the church.

As the Mayordomo waits outside on horseback, the Mayordoma and the serranas enter the church to venerate the paso of the cross sitting to the right of the alter.

The romería circles the Cross of the Llano.

Preparing for the romería of Santa Eulalia. A traditionally dressed horseman watches as final preparations are made for a couple on muleback. Women, whether on mule or horseback, dress in "gypsy" costumes.

Small, but beautifully gilded and painted statues, such as this one of Santa
Eulalia were common before their mass destruction during the turmoil of the
Civil War years.

Dancing, singing, and drinking are the activities which entertain the people as they await the mounted procession at the halfway point in the romería route.

Male followers of the saint collectively fight the bull in the ring at Santa Eulalia.

Traditional washing in the river on the morning of the second day at Santa Eulalia.

In the shelter of a temporary bar, followers of the saint take time out from the dancing and singing on the second day.

After twenty-four hours, the singing and drinking continues.

Led by the Mayordomos and officers of the brotherhood, the **paso of Santa Eulalia** is carried in a procession on the second day.

An emotion charged moment on the last day. The silver staff of the present Mayordomo is transferred to the Mayordomo of the coming year.

Preparation of an image of a patron saint for an aldea procession.

Rites and Rituals

SECTION III

In Almonaster itself, corporateness is reified, reaffirmed and "invigorated" through a process of ritual competition and cooperation. In this largest and most complex of the communities, periods of competition and cooperation are separated in time, but both of these forces are active within the same community; there is virtually no sense of competition or cooperation with a similar outside social entity. During this crucial ritual period, the multicommunity is the effective social universe. Thus it would be difficult to conceive of competition from another community since Almonaster is the dominant community in the system, at least in its own eyes. In a very real sense, the process of maintaining corporateness in Almonaster is the exception for the multicommunity, not the rule. In this chapter, the reaffirmation of corporateness through the ritual process in the small communities that surround Almonaster is the subject. The process among these small communities is analogous to that in Almonaster but not the same. Competition and cooperation both take place but to different degrees and by different social entities.

CHAPTER 4

Competition and Cooperation: Festival Cycle in the Multicommunity

In Almonaster the festivals, and the sodalities that run them, are means of marking and reaffirming boundaries between social organizational entities. Furthermore each of these entities, or communities, by the enactment of rituals, reifies and reaffirms its basic corporateness. The problem when dealing with the multicommunity is that such a concept proposes two kinds of group identity and solidarity; that is, two levels of corporateness, in at least a social sense. The first, and most powerful, is on the level of the individual community. The second, and less powerful, is the level of the multicommunity.[1]

Distinctions between these two levels of corporateness are most readily apparent in the rituals of the multicommunity. During the following discussion it should be remembered that the annual festivals are symbols of corporateness, that they are ways for the individuals involved to reaffirm and remind themselves of basic underlying cultural and social forces. As such they serve as indicators. The full dynamics of corporateness or of multicommunity cannot be understood without reference to the "pragmatic" areas of life for which the rituals are only vague symbols. Thus economics, status and wealth, world view, to point out only the grossest of heuristic categories, are all areas which must be considered before a definitive understanding can be reached. The rituals do not create, but rather reaffirm, reify and "rekindle" preexisting states.

FIESTAS PATRONALES: COMPETITION AND COOPERATION IN THE ALDEAS

The major, and often only, community festival of note in the aldeas is the celebration of the Patron Saint of the village. These fiestas take place from the end of June to the end of October. Most are held in the six weeks from the middle of July to the end of August. This scheduling of the festivals coincides with the height of the grain harvesting season and is indicative of the role of the Saint in the agriculture of the village. A Patron watches over the village, keeping the inhabitants safe and healthy. The quality of the harvest is the Patron's domain and it is obvious that one of the functions of the ritual is the increase of the land and thanksgiving for the bounty of the Saint. Part of each festival is dedicated to the veneration of the Patron Saint by the people of the community.

The veneration of the Saint is marked by cooperation among the members of the community. But veneration of the Saint is only half of the festival. The other half, the secular part of the festival, requires the cooperation of the group in order to better compete with the surrounding villages. In the competition, one village outdoes another by putting on a better secular ritual than the other. The secular part of the festival is meant to attract people from all of the surrounding villages. There are dances, games and bars. Ideally the village that gives the best party is the "winner." But with no impartial judges, each village must decide for itself how it has done.

In considering the competition between villages, it is important to remember that it takes the form of entertaining guests (though they pay for it). In the aldeas the value of being pueblerino is evident in the strong positive sanction on hospitality toward visitors. This often extends beyond simple friendliness to food and drink. At the same time the simpler social structure of the aldeas creates less tension. Both of these factors militate against competition taking the form of hostility or aggression.

Fiesta Structure

The organization of the festival is normally in the hands of the Directiva of the hermandad of the patron saint. The Directiva is usually chosen every year by its predecessors from among the other hermanos, and normally every permanent member of the village is a member of the hermandad. The composition, number and titles of the Directiva vary from village to village. The head positions are always held by successful men. Often this two or three man Comisión is the only leadership. These people not only take active parts in the religious ritual of the festival, but also are responsible for the organization and funding of the secular festivities. They usually organize lotteries, raffles, and winter dances to raise funds which, along with membership dues, help to pay for decorations, fireworks, prizes, and bands. Often admission is charged to the dances which may be held each evening of the festival. Publicity is also arranged by the Comisión in the form of handbills and posters which are circulated throughout the area.

The schedule of events at a Patron Saint festival is a standard one. Larger or richer aldeas may elaborate on it, but the basic pattern remains the same. There are four days of ritual which are timed to fall on or near the Saint's Day. Table 4-1 summarizes these four days including common elaborations and necessary ritual elements.

Relatively few aldeas do more than the "necessary" ritual. When they do elaborate, it is always in the larger aldeas, both because of the greater amount of money and the greater number of residents. Most aldeas rely heavily on the attendance of outsiders at the secular parts of the ritual because their numbers maintain the festive atmosphere, and their money at the bars and in the dance entrance fees are the main sources of income for the hermandad.

The "necessary" ritual begins on the first evening with the Rosary. This is a kind of notification to the saint from the people that his veneration is about to begin. In all but one aldea, this in the only activity on this night. It is an activity for the hermandad, the community, only. It is not closed to outsiders but not important to them either, certainly not worth a long trip by foot or bicycle. Even in the aldea which holds a dance on this night, attendance by outsiders is sparse. The secular festivities are not really underway and people who spend only one day at a festival do not choose to come on this "slow" night.

The second day is often divided into two quite distinct parts. The "necessary" ritual of this day is the most important from the point of view of intracommunity cooperation. This is the mass and procession, the high point of religious ritual. In the evening following this mass and procession there is very often a dance, though again it is not the really "big" dance of the celebration and is not well attended by outsiders. The division between these two ritual events is most apparent in terms of the people who are present in each instance. Outsiders are rarely present during the religious ritual; not because they would be unwelcome but because they have no reason to want to come. This image of the Saint is the

TABLE 4-1 Patron Saint Festival Elements

Day	*Necessary Ritual Elements*	*Optional Elaborations*
Day 1	Evening group recitation of the Rosary in honor of the Saint. Setting up of the Saint's image in the chapel area. Rockets. Cooperation.	May be accompanied by tamborilero and done during a procession. Dances may be held before and after.
Day 2	Procession of Saint's image and mass. Priest. Rockets. Held in the morning or evening. Naming of the Comisión for the coming year almost always follows at the end of the procession. Cooperation.	A morning mass and procession may be followed in the afternoon and evening by games, trapshoots, dances and fireworks. Evening mass and procession may be followed by dances and fireworks. Processions may be accompanied by tamborilero.
Day 3	Secular festivities: games and dances. Cooperation of in-group in Competition with other villages.	Fireworks, trapshoots, dance contests, crowning of "Queen" of the festival.
Day 4	Return of the Saint to customary place, the first act of the new Comisión. Rockets. Cooperation.	May be accomplished in a procession. Dances.

Patron of this aldea only. Even when the same saint is Patron of another aldea, those poeple do not feel any special relation to any but their own image of the saint. This parochialism mirrors the overt reason for the mass and procession: the veneration of this particular image of a Saint, who is responsible for the well-being of these people. There is a collective patron/client relationship between the people and the Saint. This ritual is the people's duty toward a Saint whose duty is their protection throughout the year.

The mass is given by the priest who comes out from Almonaster. It usually takes place in the one-room school house as many aldeas do not have chapels. The women, children, and girls usually fill the room while the men and older boys wait outside the door. As soon as the mass is over, the image of the saint is brought out of the school house and set on a small paso. This is the right and duty of the comisión. In many aldeas traditionally a tamborilero accompanies the procession. Along with the priest, he is the only other outsider present.

As the procession goes over the main streets of the aldea, the important ritual element of rockets is ever present; thus "a procession with great salvos of rockets" is a common phrase to indicate a really admirable procession. In some aldeas men augment the rockets by firing their shotguns in the air, though this is frowned upon by the Guàrdia Civil. As the image passes through the village, those who have waited at home to greet the procession or those who have run ahead to greet it from their doorstep, throw wheat or rice onto the paso as they cheer: *"Viva La Virgen de Fatima, Querida!"* ("Hurray for the beloved Virgin of Fatima"), or whoever the Patron happens to be. *"Viva, Los Mayordomos"* or *"la Comisión."* *"Viva quien la lleva!"* (Hurray for those who carry her!"). And on occasion, a polite *"Viva el paroco,"* ("Hurray for the priest") can be heard. From the procession itself the same cheers ring out, redoubled when a housewife throws wheat or flower petals.

The importance of the ritual is underscored not only by the offerings of "first fruits," but also by the fact that it is the only procession in the aldea in which women traditionally take turns along with the men in carrying the paso. This represents the height of community cooperation. On occasion there are people from other aldeas, and even Almonaster, present; but these people only heighten the in-group identity fostered by the rite. These visitors are almost universally former aldea members who have "come home" for the Patron's festival. There is a common feeling that this is an important time for the family to be together. Additionally, many people also tend to view the relationship between the Saint and the individual as a tie which, though kindled by residence, is not broken by a change of residence. Thus someone from the aldea who moves to another community may often continue to consider himself in a patron/client relationship with the saint of his former residence, at the same time that he is in a relationship with a new saint.

The tight solidarity of the community is quite evident, especially to residents of the town of Almonaster. Coming from the relative sophistication of the town, they always comment with awe on the *"mejor ambiente aquí que en el pueblo,"* ("the better atmosphere here than in the town").

The procession returns to the schoolhouse and the Hermano Mayor hands a note to the priest which gives the names of the Comisión for the coming year. Until this moment, the names of the new Comisión members has been a closely guarded secret of the present Comisión. In some of the smaller and poorer aldeas, the men named for the coming year are miners or other salaried workers who only come home a few times during the year. They complain that they will be away too much to carry out their charge effectively. In the crowd others comment to each other that the Comisión named these men because of their greater affluence. The crowd sympathizes, for all of the overt and covert reasons, with the newly named men, but no one doubts that they will make the sacrifice. Their rather public display of dissatisfaction attests to the closeness of the entire group.

The third day is the high point of competition between aldeas. Each village hopes that its secular rituals will overwhelm the visitors from other aldeas. Not only is it important that many outsiders come on this day to be "given a better time here than they can give others in their own festival," but also that they spend the money that is so necessary to the funding of the festival. Aside from the typical festival drinking and merrymaking, there are three activities that no Patron Saint festival would be without. These special events start in the afternoon with a kind of "warm up" in the form of a "sack race," often combined with catching a loose chicken, to get people into a festive mood. The participants are young boys, normally all from the aldea, and the chicken is the prize. This amusing spectacle is entertainment for everyone. The next event is a special bicycle race which attracts boys and even young men from all of the aldeas in the area.

The *"Carrera de Cintas"* is a customary competition which used to be done on donkey back, now always on bicycles. It represents the combined efforts of the unmarried girls in the community toward the success of the festival, for they are responsible for making the *cintas*, or "ribbons." In the "Ribbon Race" the object is for each rider to win as many ribbons as possible. At the end of the race, the rider with the most ribbons wins a prize. Each ribbon is about a yard long and about three inches wide. It is often heavily embroidered and then signed in embroidery by the girl who made it. At one end is a short fringe, and attached to the other is a metal ring about an inch in diameter. The ribbons are wound around short sections of bamboo and strung across the street on a wire about seven feet off the ground. Each ribbon is affixed to the tube of bamboo in such a way that if the ring is pulled, it will unwind and come off.

The riders start from about 50 to 75 yards away and one at a time they attempt to win a ribbon. Each rider carries a stick about the size of a lead pencil. Riding at top speed, they are supposed to skewer the ring with the stick. This is quite difficult. The crowd won't let them go slowly, so that it is all they can do to keep from falling as they stretch to reach the wire. A success is immediately apparent as the rider passes the wire with the ribbon streaming behind him. The riders continue to take turns until all the ribbons have been won. Each rider ties the ribbons he wins to his arms or his bicycle so that the best riders are readily apparent. Although people root for the riders from their home town, this competition is general entertainment for the crowd, not really competition between communities.

The third and most important activity of the day is the dance, in which everyone participates. Some participate by entering the fenced in and decorated dance area; others by sitting around the outside at the tables set up for the liquor stands. In the aldeas that have no electricity, the band is made up of saxophone and other assorted brass, and an accordion. This style band cannot match the prestige of a modern electrified one with electric guitars and an electric organ. The difference in fees is not a problem, but the presence or absence of electricity is. Electricity is itself a point of prestige for the aldea. Nonetheless, the dance and the atmosphere around it are the key points in the competition, and an aldea without electricity may have a dance *"con mucho ambiente"* that outshines the electrified dance of another village. The success of a dance in the aldeas, most of which average about 130 inhabitants, depends on the number of single girls in the aldea. Young men come to the dance from outside if the aldea is known to have single girls, and it is the single couples which take the lead. A dance of largely married couples is a sedate, less than exciting affair. When the aldea has only a very few single girls, it is assumed beforehand that the festival will be disappointing.

Visitors very rarely stay over night, so that on the fourth day the ritual is again attended only by the people of the community. The ceremony of replacement of the saint in its normal place is short. There are cheers for the new Comisión, but there is little of the fervor which marked the procession of the second day.

With the festival over, the people of the aldea may settle back and watch what kind of show other aldeas put on. Most people will only go to the festivals of the closest aldeas. Young married couples go farther on occasion in a car or truck if there is one in the aldea. The single boys are the ones who go farthest and who are the chief informants at home about the quality of festivities in the multicommunity.

The sense of competition that the people of the aldeas have is not really one of "winning" or "losing." It is rather a kind of dynamic balance. The competition itself is a natural state without a beginning or ending. Two common metaphors are used to express the relationship between communities. That of "one family; the children always measure themselves against one another but they are also very close." The other is the "one town" metaphor; "Each aldea is like a street in the town. They hope to outdo the other streets, but they are also united." Certainly the rivalry is a function of the sense of common identity and not vice versa. The causes of unity are many, but there is one overriding symbol of the unity. That is the Romería of Santa Eulalia.

SANTA EULALIA, THE PATRONESS OF A MULTICOMMUNITY: FURTHER FUNCTIONS OF A FESTIVAL

The Romería of Santa Eulalia is not simply a festival for the town of Almonaster, however central townsmen may be in the hermandad. In almost every aldea there are members of the hermandad. The prevalence of pictures of Santa Eulalia, of the singing of fandangos of Santa Eulalia, and of vicarious participation in the ritual by all, give further indication of the stature of the saint in the aldeas. In terms of actual participation, only a few of the aldea dwellers are present at Santa Eulalia in any one year. Yet the yearly festival is important to everyone. Everyone knows when it is being held and hopes some day to go. Many adults have gone at least once in their lives.

Santa Eulalia, aside from being a patron saint to the multicommunity, is a symbol of the organic solidarity or symbiotic relationship between member communities. For those who live in the aldeas, the festival could not go on without the active participation of the people from the town of Almonaster. At the same time, the people of Almonaster feel a duty to the aldea dwellers. They realize that Santa Eulalia is the patron of all. In terms of the actual ermita and the land at Santa Eulalia, it is legally as much the property of the aldeas as it is of the town. Just as the ermita is neutral ground in terms of the Crosses, it is also neutral in terms of the aldeas. Here the people of the multicommunity meet in cooperative veneration of the Saint.

The manner in which each group cooperates in Santa Eulalia is indicative not only of the relationship between all the communities, but also of the nature of the communities. Most of the communities in the multicommunity are in a very asymmetrical relationship with the town, in terms of this festival as well as in the more "pragmatic" areas of life. In this case, townspeople tend to emerge as a distinct part of the festival group; in contrast, the people from the various aldeas tend to merge. Their aldea identities blend into a generalized non-town category. While the aldea people do not generally take major parts in the actual ritual in that when they march in the procession, they are not chosen to carry banners or other ritual paraphernalia, nevertheless they are participants. One or two aldeas have begun to approach Almonaster in size and complexity which means that the relationship between Almonaster and the aldeas is not strictly asymmetrical and that the people from the aldea wish to maintain a separate group identity within the ritual. In this situation, cooperation still is the theme, but the "individuality" within the ritual is an incipient form of competition.

El Patrás is the clearest example of an aldea which has crossed a crucial size and complexity Rubicon. It plays an individualized part within the ritual. Other than Almonaster itself, this is the only community which formally enters the ritual area in Romería. People from El Patrás enter separately on horseback, and they ritually greet the Saint and assembled people by circling the ermita. Although they have a role which is clearly secondary to Almonaster itself and they are not officially considered a second hermandad, their actions clearly state their independent stance. In terms of size, El Patrás is one of the two largest aldeas.[1] The other large aldea, Veredas, has no individual identity within the ritual, even though it is even larger than El Patrás. This dissimilarity is due to the different levels of socioeconomic complexity in the two aldeas. Though numerically large, Veredas is much simpler than Patrás. Most of its families are minifundia subsistence farmers with a minimal cash economy, and many are agricultural laborers. Only a few people in Veredas are traditional cash crop farmers, the "middle class" of agriculturalists. Additionally, the aldea has no landowner-class agriculturalists nor major businessmen. El Patrás, on the other hand, has one major businessman and the highest number of "middle class" farmers outside of the town itself. At the same time, Patrás has a large number of men employed in the mines who commute daily from the aldea. This large resident population of miners is, in aldea terms, quite affluent.

In spite of the differences in participation, the festival is as important to one group as to the others. The ritual data supplied in the previous chapter is as applicable to the aldea people as to the town dwellers. Thus the fandangos of Santa Eulalia are as meaningful to the aldeas as to Almonaster itself because the mention of "Almonaster," the only center of population mentioned in the songs, can mean either the "town of Almonaster" or the "término of Almonaster." Consequently when a person from the aldea of Rinconmalillo sings of Santa Eulalia that ". . . there is no one in Almonaster who doesn't carry her in his breast . . . ," the verse conveys as much meaning for the singer as it may for someone from the town itself.

In addition, the general poetic style of the fandangos of Santa Eulalia, are open to many kinds of valid interpretation. For example, the simple love song reproduced on p. 101 seems to many people to be a direct allusion to the aldea of Molares. "En tu puerta siempre un guindo . . ." does not simply mean having any cherry tree at the doorway, but refers to a specific kind of cherry, the *guinda,* for which Molares is famous. There are guinda trees in other parts of the area, but Molares is the only place "known" for them.

At the same time that Santa Eulalia represents the interrelationship between the communities, she also represents the boundary of that group and its identity in the face of the outside world. Two kinds of people come to the ritual: those from the multicommunity whose aim is to venerate the Saint and enjoy themselves, and people from without the multicommunity, "*forasteros,*" who are there to be entertained, to appreciate the ritual carried out by the insiders but who themselves may not take an active part. "Forastero" is a term applied to any Spaniard who is not from the multicommunity. Although everyone is very happy to see more and more forasteros come to Santa Eulalia for both the money and prestige, the distinction remains a very important one. The ritual of Santa Eulalia represents not only the corporateness of the multicommunity, but also the principal corporate property of the multicommunity.

To understand Santa Eulalia as corporate property requires an awareness of certain general patterns in Spain, particularly the way in which most Romerías of note are organized. The famous Romerías of Spain usually are held by groups of hermandades, rather than by only one as in the case of Almonaster. Normally one of the hermandades, or the hermandades from one particular town or city, are considered to be the "oldest" or the "real" or "original" holders of the Romería. The rest are newcomers and their number often increases. To join, the new hermandades must pay money to the founding hermandades. This is a direct economic benefit to the Romería. Secondly, they insure an increase in the number of spectators and participants which means more money spent by individuals during the actual festival, which is another real benefit to the Romería and the hermandades. If an hermandad has a Romería and they need money, as they always do, allowing secondary hermandades to join is the best method of making the Romería solvent. Money for Santa Eulalia is a constant necessity; there is never enough. Among the local forasteros who have been coming for years to the Romería, there are some very wealthy contingents from the rich mining términos just to the south of the término of Almonaster. Each year groups from these towns make overtures to the hermandad asking that they be allowed to form secondary hermandades of Santa Eulalia. They promise rich additions to the festival as well as pledges of recognition of Almonaster as the head hermandad. In spite of genuine money troubles, Almonaster steadfastly denies entrance to the corporation by the forasteros. This rejection of the offer of the forasteros is a clear case of "the irrational economic behavior of peasants," except for the fact that the spokesmen for the multicommunity, the directiva of the hermandad, represents the most sophisticated businessmen and administrators in Almonaster, people who are quite aware of the economic benefits which such a merger would bring. By refusing to share the expense of the pilgrimage, Santa Eulalia remains a body of ritual which all member communities may take part in, even to the point of organizing a de facto romería from Patrás, but which excludes all outsiders from active participation.

RITUALS AND SODALITIES: STRUCTURAL BOUNDARIES

Throughout the multicommunity the major festivals of the annual cycle emerge as basic cultural landmarks. The differences which may be perceived in the festivals, from one community to the next, are always differences of degree rather than of kind. Overall, the major function of the ritual remains the same from the greatest to the smallest of the communities. Similarly, the basic process is the same from one to the next. The festival presents sanctioned channels for venting repressed hostility and tension arising from the inevitable interpersonal conflicts which arise from the conduct of normal interpersonal relations. This emotional energy is expended through in-group cooperation and inter-group competition in the rituals. This in-group cooperation and inter-group competition promotes integration and group identity. The symbolism of the rituals closely follows this basic theme as it reifies the unity and corporateness of the group. Membership in these groups is based on residence; thus the social dimensions of the group are directly coupled to discrete physical areas and features. In fact, these physical features of the group become major symbols within the ritual. Consequently the net result of the rituals is the decrease of potentially disruptive tension and increased integration of the system. This is expressed by the reification and reaffirmation of the social and spatial identity of the group.

Important differences in the festivals do appear in terms of the amount of intensity of emotional energy which is produced by the communities at different levels of sociocultural complexity. This difference in available energy can be seen in both the nature and duration of in-group cooperation and the intensity of inter-group competition within the ritual context. As sociocultural complexity and numbers increase, so does the amount of in-group hostility to be dissipated by participation in ritual activities. Almonaster with a considerably larger population and dramatically more complex sociocultural composition exhibits a much higher degree of energy than any of the aldeas. In Almonaster, the competitive phase, which takes place within the community for lack of another equal "opponent" in the rest of the multicommunity, is noted for the amount of overtly expressed hostility. The competition of an average aldea is, in contrast, almost never characterized by any display of intergroup hostility. The cooperative phase in Almonaster is many weeks long and rather intense as opposed to the relaxed, short-term cooperation which goes into one of the aldea patron saint festivals.

The Cross of May, Santa Eulalia, and the Patron Saint festivals of the aldeas are the only festivals in the annual cycle which serves these specific functions; that is, the maintenance of social identity and group boundaries. They are also the only festivals which are characterized by a specific ritual social structure of their own, the sodality, which though they are symbolic of the every day social structure of the group, are actually distinct and specific to the ritual context. Although membership is purely voluntary, the hermandades, the sodalities, always include all members of the group as followers of their titular deity. This specialized structural principle is needed in this case to organize the high degree of in-group cooperation and inter-group competition which are characteristic of both preparation and actual performance of the rituals.

Competition, in which the entire group acts as one side in opposition to other units, is a key part of the process by which the group's corporate identity emerges. In the término of Almonaster this competition between groups is not a random one. The universe of opponents is bounded and, taken collectively, the member units of this universe form a higher, but analogous, level of structure. This higher level, that of multicommunity, has its own annual festival of integration, and physical and social identity, quite analogous to the festival of the individual member communities. Thus each community has one set of rituals to express its identity with respect to a group of "like" units. In this case each community is by turns performer and audience in a competitive system that finds in each performance of the individual community festival one-half of the actual contest. Each community is also part of a second annual festival in which competitors are all aligned in one segmented group which collectively performs the ritual for an audience of "generalized others." The positive effect of competition on the multicommunity level is possible only because of the peoples' experience of actual competition on the inter-community level. Actual competition on the multicommunity level, without this knowledge of what "real" competition is like, would not materialize, since in the absence of a well-defined audience the ritual is characterized by cooperation of the multicommunity in-group. The sense of competition is present as a symbolic factor which finds the multicommunity opposed to an ill-defined "other" category; hardly the kind of opposition that by itself promotes highly charged partisan feelings.

Analysis of these rituals of corporateness as performed at different levels within the same multicommunity has been sufficient to demonstrate that although the same general process is active in each community, the traditional cultural vehicle for the process may vary. Hence the meaning of the Patron Saint festivals of the aldeas is not the same as the Patron Saint festival of the town. The key factor in this difference is the presence of socioculturally equal competition. This competition is a basic part of the process of reaffirmation, reification and general maintenance of community identity and integration. The entire system of Patron Saint festivals in the aldeas affords the vehicle for this competition. The town, because of its more complex sociocultural profile, is unable to participate actively in this competitive system. Hence the town's Patron Saint festival does not fulfill the same function as the others in the multicommunity. Instead, the town must create its own internal competition in a more complex set of rituals. The Patron Saint festival is apparently less suited to this end than the Cross of May ritual.[2]

The historical implication clearly is that the complex festival cycle of the town developed as the situation for ritual competition with another community waned. This is supported by local tradition which states that there was a time when the Cross of the Fuente was the only one in the town. This fact is accepted by both hermandades and cited by both as the reason for calling the Fuente, "the real Cross." The rise of a second cross may have coincided with the end of a traditional rivalry between Almonaster and Cortegana. Local tradition holds that this competition between Almonaster and Cortegana took place during a Romería in honor of San Cristóbal. The site of the Romería was the top of the mountain which overlooks Almonaster. Tradition states that there was always a procession from Almonaster and one from Cortegana. Conflict slowly escalated and coincident with territorial disputes, finally reached overt hostilities which caused the end of the Romería. Today all that remains is the ruined bullring and the vestiges of the foundation of an ermita. The assumption is that at the time of this romería, Almonaster was afforded competition either during the romería itself or that its Patron Saint festival was part of a cycle in which, at least, Cortegana joined.[3]

Although careful study of the festivals indicates similar processes in the various communities of the multicommunity, such study reveals very little about either the internal structure of the community or the related factors which create the basis for the ritual. Interpretation of the symbolism and general style of the ritual depends on foreknowledge of each case. Even given the sharp difference between the actual style and presentation of the rituals in the town as opposed to the countryside, the ritual period is the time at which the communities are most similar. The ritual is certainly more standardized than the everyday reality of the communities. The study of festivals can tell what they do, and how they do it, but not why. The most important information to be gained from the study of the annual festivals is the delineation of structural entities basic to the life of the society, within which the lives of the people are organized. They live in various communities and these are basic, conscious, corporate-tending units of social organization.

In the internal structure and organization of these various units lies the true genesis of the rituals, the conditions which lead to the identity and solidarity, to the general corporate nature that is reified and reaffirmed by the ritual. In part, the rituals are their own cause. Taken in diachronic perspective, the folk explanation of *"es costumbre,"* "it is custom" is a valid expression of the rituals as their own cause. But this is a minor part of the "Why?" of the rituals. The same is true for the very generalized explanation of ritual as the excape valve for energy generated by the application of a system of values by a group. The real "Why?" involves the very mundane and individually trivial conditions and behaviors of everyday life within each community and between each of the communities. An explanation of the rituals on the ground that the town is more complex, that its ritual symbolizes the organic solidarity which other communities lack, or that each aldea is bound into the multicommunity by very practical considerations of which Santa Eulalia is only a symbol is not enough. The rituals supply the barest of structural outlines. The internal composition of the communities, and the forces which hold each in its position in the constellation of the multicommunity, are a more comprehensive explanation and are the subject of a future book on Santa Eulalia.

NOTES

[1]Since the average size of the sixteen aldeas is about 17.6% of that of the town, or about 141 inhabitants, El Patrás' 318 inhabitants constitute a center of population about 40% the total size of the town. Of the sixteen aldeas, only two actually exceed 26% of the size of the town's population. El Patrás is one, and Veredas, at 54%, is the other (all figures are from the 1966 census).

[2]The Cross is venerated in many parts of Spain and with many kinds of ritual. An interesting parallel to Almonaster might be Bonares, a city of five thousand, in Southern Huelva. Bonares has twelve crosses and twelve hermandades. Each year a different hermandad is in charge of the ritual and their cross is the central cross for that year's ritual (Masegui, 1969:4).

[3]In 1791 Almonaster was the seat of a vicarage which included, in addition to nearby Cortegana, El Cerro del Andevalo (472 vecinos), Santa Ana La Real (123 vecinos), El Jabugo (163 vecinos), La Nava (57 vecinos), Aroche (425 vecinos), Cortegana (442 vecinos), Almonaster (472 vecinos). This information comes from, *Plan y decreto de ereción y dotación* de curatos del Arzobispado de Sevilla, Año 1791.

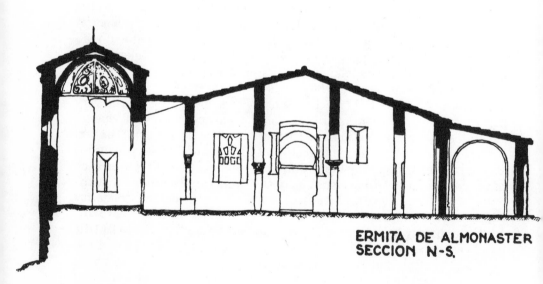

ERMITA DE ALMONASTER
SECCION N-S.

CHAPTER 5

Conclusion: Community, Multicommunity and the Ritual Process

While the study of the ritual of the multicommunity cannot explain the genesis of social relationships, or of values and other cultural artifacts, it can demonstrate the identities and boundaries of social organization, and it can demonstrate the mediation of paradoxes between the cultural and social orders.

In the first chapter three paradoxes were introduced, paradoxes which are mediated for Almuñenses so that they may perceive and live both as reality. The two points of view involved in each paradox are equally valid as parts of a description of the multicommunity of Almonaster. Santa Eulalia's people live complex lives in a complex social and cultural matrix. The ritual system mediates the complexity of life and maintains its order. By doing so, real complexity can never become chaos or paradox for individual human beings who must somehow live unified lives.

Looking at the first paradox, "What is it about Almonaster which has enabled Almuñenses to hold on to the 'good life,' in spite of difficult material conditions, while so many of those around them seem to have lost so much?" A variety of ecological and demographic factors do exist as preconditions for Almonaster's success, but more important in this context are the mechanisms and conditions which culture and social organization provide to make that success a reality. Here the central

135

mechanism is the ritual process which generates the conditions necessary for group identity and corporate control over culture. Almonaster is exceptional in the region for the amount of "traditional culture," especially ritual structure, which is still practiced. In contrast, the most depressed neighboring populations are those where ritual life has literally ceased to exist.

Almonaster's ritual system, group corporateness, and identity do not directly improve the individual Almuñense standard of living; rather they maintain the social and psychological support engendered by a "healthy," fully functioning sociocultural system. The ritual system not only preserves social order and dependability, but also aids in the local definition of goals, values, and standards of living because of the high degree of cultural homogeneity and corporate control over cultural systems which the communities uphold. The ritual process which maintains sociocultural structure allows the multicommunity to adapt to its wider socioeconomic environment in a protective way. The Almuñenses live in a community culture which sets standards of consumption, goals, and values, which are predicated on the social and economic conditions found locally. When a woman sees a self-cleaning oven on the television in the bar, she laughs—not because it is unattainable, but because it is unthinkable to desire it in the context of the local culture and society in which she lives. Nor is her position in society, her sense of value and contribution, predicated on such "nonsense." Although she is certainly interested in prosperity and personal social progress, these things are defined by the local system and though still difficult to attain, they are not perceived as impossible.[1]

As local units in other areas become less and less bounded, as identity and corporateness are dissipated, people become parts of the wider "national" system. For most of them goals and aspirations can no longer be achieved in the local community context and they move away, drawn to the cities and to industry. Even when such emigrants send money home, it is often no help in maintaining local sociocultural organization. Consequently the local system, which is torn and malfunctioning, ceases to support those who are left behind. This condition is a viscious and downward cycle into which Almuñenses have not yet entered.

When individual villages have failed, the survivors have become incorporated into one of the remaining villages or into the town itself. Even in the villages which persist, people do leave but not in overwhelming numbers. They are the ones who have left the multicommunity for the city, the mine, and the factory. In the eyes of those who remain behind, these emigrants are victims because although they may prosper economically, they have left the social and cultural context which makes life "good." Many of those who have left repeat this perception both in word and in actions. They do this by coming home to visit during the festivals which reify their home community's social and physical identity, drawing strength from their home to face their life in the "modern world."

Looking at the second paradox, the simultaneous perception of life as being wholly egalitarian and wholly hierarchical, we recognize that both points of view combine to describe Almonaster. In life these two ideals exist simultaneously but are segregated so that they appear in different contexts and so that they are applied by each individual to himself and to others in a highly ordered and systematic way. But segregation and order must be periodically reaffirmed, for the communities find themselves nested in a wider socioeconomic system which would depress egalitarianism and elevate hierarchicalism.

Clearly the ritual system does more than simply remind people that both views are supposed to be equal in value and equally current in community culture. The function of the rituals is to allow this cultural verity to be maintained as social reality. In this case the dialectic between the two is such a powerful reality that the ritual system can only reify and mediate between the two by considering each in a separate part of the ritual cycle and by carefully releasing the tension which has been created anew since the end of the last cycle a year before. Hence, the competitive ritual between the Crosses and the rivalry between the Patron Saint festivals of the villages both stress egalitarianism. The dialectic of egalitarianism versus hierarchicalism creates the energy released and channeled during these rituals. With egalitarianism reinstated in the minds and the behavior of the people, the cooperative ritual of Santa Eulalia then reaffirms the hierarchical dimension of community and multicommunity. In Santa Eulalia hierarchicalism is reinforced in two forms: the relationship between individual statuses and roles and the superordination of Almonaster, the town, over the subordinant village communities. Hierarchicalism has thus been restated as a necessary element of the multicommunity and its relative position with respect to egalitarianism strengthened. Thus the lines of segregation between these two cultural forms have again been finely drawn. The order of culture and social organization has been reaffirmed in the minds of Santa Eulalia's people.

The last paradox (how does Almonaster manage the almost superhuman feat of living up to formalidad?) has been answered as a function of the ritual process. This analysis is not meant to prove that Almuñenses love each other, nor that conscious bad feelings towards others disappear after the ritual. Indeed, nothing could be farther from the truth. What has happened is the dissipation of unconscious tensions and the reaffirmation of the rule which says that one should not *express* interpersonal hostility. Personal enmity remains, but it is again controllable and no longer exists as friction which would slow down the harmonious movement of the social order.

The final question asked in the introduction was, "What is Almonaster and how does it work?" An implicit assumption which I have tried to demonstrate is that the social organization of the community and multicommunity is a cyclical phenomenon which moves from order to disorder and back to order again. The mechanism which recreates order out of disorder is the ritual system. The ritual process, in this case, demands the interaction of a set of groups which share culture to the extent that they are all able to participate in the same bounded ritual system. Thus the multicommunity of Almonaster is most powerful and most obvious at this level of environmental adaptation. Social change finds its roots in the non-ritual period I have characterized as disorder (perhaps more exactly, the period in which the system is losing order), in response to social, demographic and ecological reality. In even the most stable of systems these real changes will influence the order which is being reified/recreated during the ritual phase. As social reality from the period of disorder is incorporated into the ritualized order, it becomes part of the cultural system and exerts a progressive influence on subsequent social relationships. Thus the fluorescent lights and plastic flowers of the Cross of the Fuente typify the symbolic incorporation of such a process of sociocultural change.

A MODEL OF RITUAL PROCESS
AND
COMMUNITY CLASSIFICATION

Although I have tried throughout to let ethnographic detail and analysis speak for themselves, it is now necessary to consider the multicommunity ritual system in the more general terms of the theoretical model which best describes it. This theoretical discussion is necessary if we are to generalize from the specific ethnographic case of Almonaster, in which the ritual system is the culturally prescribed form of expression of the Principle of Group Maintenance, to some synthetic form which may justly be included in a model of community and multicommunity.

Of the several famous models of ritual process, the one which most clearly fits this ethnographic reality is that of Gregory Bateson's Schismogenesis. Bateson's model (1958:176-177) posits two forms of ritualized interaction which alternate to maintain a dynamic equilibrium within the system. In one form, called Symmetrical Schismogenesis, competitive conditions are produced between culturally defined like units. Left unchecked, this condition leads inevitably to fission of the system into separate but equal parts. In effect, ingroup identity and corporateness renewed in this phase becomes too strong, making intergroup relations impossible. This tendency toward fission is offset by Complementary Schismogenesis, a phase characterized by the cooperative relations between culturally defined unequal units (that is, interaction which recognizes the basic asymmetry of status and participation of roles and / or groups). But left unchecked, this form of schismogenesis will lead to the fusion of the subordinate part into the dominant part with a consequent loss of identity of the subordinate part as a distinguishable entity. The Symmetrical phase then follows to check this negative aspect of Complementary Schismogenesis.

According to this interpretation of the model, the rituals of the Crosses and the village Patron Saints can be seen as two different and excellent examples of symmetrical schismogenesis. Santa Eulalia with her town segment and her village segment may be seen as complementary schismogenesis. Together these rituals reify the complex structure of the multicommunity social organization.

In both phases of schismogenesis at the group level, one factor is prominent. That is the differentiation in culture specific terms of like and unlike (asymmetrical) units. Herein lies an important clue to the actual structural form of the communities maintained by the ritual system. Considering the kinds of systems presented by different types of communities, it is clear that some occur in systems in which there are culturally defined like units and others inhabit systems in which they have no such culturally defined counterparts. Examples of communities without equals in their own systems are the many "closed corporate communities" (Wolf 1955) reported in the literature, and the more open and complex communities such as Almonaster, the town, which find themselves in systems including several communities none of which are recognized as their equal. The alternative possibility, systems in which communities have equals, exists among the satellite communities of Almonaster. In the latter case the form of the identity and harmony generating group is simple and straight forward; the community and the symmetrical schismogenic group are isomorphic. In this case each community is in competitive and cooperative relations with its neighbors, each contributing, by its existence, to the identity and harmony of the other.

The case of the community which inhabits a sociocultural system without equals is more complex.[2] If the assumption is accepted that competition between culturally defined equal groups is essential to identity and harmony, then the hypothesis would be that there are two alternatives for a community which has no equals: (1) lacking equal units in the same sociocultural system, the community loses identity, and ingroup hostility and aggression increases; or, (2) lacking equal units within the system, the community creates such a situation within its own membership as more or less permanent institutions. That is, internal segmentation takes place.[3] In Spain and Latin America this is almost always in the form of religious brotherhoods and/or barrio divisions. Thus, communities may be classified as Segmented or Unsegmented. Unsegmented communities are always found within a sociocultural system that includes other communities which are culturally defined as equal; Segmented communities are only found in systems in which they have no equals. Unsegmented communities are thus found in some form of multicommunity system. Segmented communities may be independent or may be a central part of a multicommunity.

In the application of the schismogenic model of community ritual process, there is a danger of assuming that the presence or absence of such process depends upon the existence of *religious* ritual. Although the presence of religious ritual is true of the Almonaster case, it is not essential to the model. Schismogenic behavior at the group level may be expressed in the *ritualization* of a wide variety of activities such as sports or economic/market relations.

One point not included in Bateson's model is the need to ritualize and thereby reify the basic cultural unity of individuals and groups who participate in the schismogenic process. As I have described it, Semana Santa performs this function in the multicommunity. To state that such a ritual is necessary does not tamper with Bateson's original construct. His primary examples of schismogenesis came from ritualized behavior between specific relatives, where the basic fact of recognized kinship ties demonstrates the basic cultural unity of the participants. I, on the other hand, have applied the model to groups whose complex social environment makes cultural unity a less self-evident and unambiguous fact of life. At the level of groups, the concreteness of symbols and relationships such as family ties is lacking, generating the need to ritualize this more intangible relationship.

SOCIAL ORGANIZATION
VERSUS ADMINISTRATIVE DISTRICT

The exacting reader will have already arrived at the final problem: To what extent is the boundary of the multicommunity really a function of local social organization, as opposed to an adaptation to externally imposed governmental/bureaucratic forms? Certainly I have never clearly differentiated between the término of Almonaster and the multicommunity of Almonaster. They are not the same. Internal evidence suggests they are not directly related. For instance, several of the population aggregates listed as parts of the término (administrative governmental district) are not considered as parts of the multicommunity and at least two communities from neighboring terminos have been or are becoming part of the multicommunity of Almonaster.

Better use of this evidence comes from an examination of the multicommunity model from a temporal aspect; that is, what is the history of the multicommunity, how does it grow? Recognizing that growth in this sense includes both increase and decrease. At present, growth of the multicommunity takes place by the processes of fission and fusion. Thus, communities can be found which are in the process of leaving or being incorporated into the multicommunity.[4] This movement is the result of pragmatic decisions made during the period of disorder, when network relationships predicated on the role definitions of social structure dominate the lives of the people. In effect, the members of the community in question begin to shift their patterns of interaction from the central community of one multicommunity to that of another.

This social reality is transformed after time (probably not more than thirty years but certainly not less than ten) to the cultural reality of the ritual system. The process can be said to be complete when, for instance, the newcomer community begins to compete with the saint's days of the other multicommunity members and when it becomes a part of the Santa Eulalia ritual. This is the process of fusion with the multicommunity. The bond of sentiment or identity with the multicommunity follows the reality of socioeconomic integration with the multicommunity. In the case of fission, the process is reversed. The community which is in the process of leaving the multicommunity will begin a progressive reorientation of its networks away from Almonaster, but for a long time, its rituals will still be seen as part of the multicommunity system and the people will still be faithful to Santa Eulalia. Finally the reality of fission from Almonaster will be recognized by the deletion of the community from the ritual system. Ritual membership and common identity are the last to be gained and the last to be lost in multicommunity fission and fusion.

THE FUTURE OF ALMONASTER

A discussion of growth leads logically to a consideration of evolution and changes in the form of the system. What is the future of Almonaster? Will it disappear like so many societies of rural Spain or will it survive in altered form? At present the outlook is optimistic. Santa Eulalia's people want prosperity, but they want it at home. They wish to be a part of modern Spain, but they do not want to be swallowed by it. They do not cling to traditional forms but live by their own responsive and changeable social and cultural organization. So far no change has come too fast or been admitted too quickly for the system to adjust to it.

NOTES

[1]For a more specific example of this in the Almonaster context see Aguilera, 1976.

[2]"Closed Corporate" or "open" considerations being unimportant in this respect (cf. Wolf 1955).

[3]An unconscious debt is certainly owed to the writing of Murdock (1949:88-90 especially) whose segmented and unsegmented communities are quite similar to mine. I read this work as a student but did not discover the similarity until after finishing the present writing. Perhaps the closest similarity to my segmented type comes on p. 90 when he writes of " . . . internal division into factions, usually two in number." He continues: "So widespread are such factional divisions, so frequently is their number precisely two, so commonly do they oppose one another in games and other activities, and so often are their reciprocal relations marked by rivalry, boasting, and covert forms of aggression that the phenomenon seems scarcely accidental. Ethnocentrism suggests a possible common function. A dual organization of a community, or of a large social group, may provide a sort of safety valve whereby agression generated by in-group disciplines may be drained off internally in socially regulated and harmless ways instead of being translated into out-group hostility and warfare. If this highly tentative hypothesis is valid, opposing factions should be more characteristic of peaceful than of warlike communities."

Compare Freeman, 1968:483, speaking of the Spanish data in general: "Everywhere we see a sociocentrism which fosters ritual competition between different villages or between barrios of one village; we see the identification of villages or barrios with different patron saints and separate feast days . . . ."

[4]In the past Almonaster has had periods of growth marked by the creation of new communities, founded either by people from other member communities or by outsiders. The last such period was in the late nineteenth century.

The longer history of the region is the history of the *fission of the entire multicommunity* of Almonaster into a series of multicommunities, now represented by the major towns of the region. While the modern case of Patrás would seem to indicate the beginning of this same multicommunity fission process, I have chosen not to discuss this level of the model here. Thus the discussion here is confined to fission/fusion from/with the multicommunity, *not* fission and fusion *of* the multicommunity.

Glossary of Almonaster Spanish

The following is a glossary of Spanish terms which appear more than once in the text. Brackets denote literal meanings. Parentheses are used for feminine endings. All translations are given in Almonaster usage and are often different from the common dictionary meanings.

aguardiente   dry anise liquor
aldea   village; satellite agricultural community
alcalde   Mayor; the head of town and término government.
alguacil   bailiff, an ayuntamiento employee
Almuñense or Almonastereño   native of Almonaster. Almuñense is correct if one subscribes to the theory that the town's name comes from the Arabic *Al Munia*—the supposed name of the castle. Almonastereño is correct if one considers the present name as the root. There is no agreement among Almonaster dwellers about which is the correct term.
aprovecharse   to take advantage of
ayuntamiento   municipal government; the town hall
campo   countryside
capataz   foreman
Carrera de Cinta   Ribbon Race
caserío   industrial or mining hamlet
chubarba   a green holly-like plant used in certain rituals
comisión   managing committee
compadrazgo   coparentage, godfathership
compadre   cofather
comadre   comother
consejales   counselors; members of the *Ayuntamiento* council or a comisión or a directiva
diputado   deputy

directiva   directors; managing committee

era   threshing floor

feria   fair

forastero   stranger; a Spaniard from outside the multicommunity

formalidad   major adult value of self-control and strict adherence to the
   rules

gira   picnic

guiso   stew

hermandad   brotherhood, sodality

hermano (a)   brother (sister); member of a sodality

Hermano Mayor   first brother, leader of a sodality

huerta   irrigated garden

interés   selfish intent

mayordomía   annual stewardship of the sodality

mayordomo (a)   annual stewards of the sodality, always one male and
   one female

niñez   childhood

novio (a)   fiancé(e)

pandilla   gang

paso   the litter or float used in a religious procession, normally with a
   statue of a saint, etc.

pueblerino   quality of being proud of one's own community, a
   characteristic of formalidad

pueblo   town

quinto   recruit; levy of recruits

refresco   reception

regreso   return; ritual reentry of a procession

romería   pilgrimage

romero   pilgrim; rosemary

salida   exit; ritual exit of a religious procession

Semana Santa   Holy Week, Easter

serrana   mountain girl; girl dressed in regional costume

tamborilero   flute and drum player

tapa   hors d'oeuvre

término, término municipal   municipal area or boundary

villa   town, the official designation for a middle-sized center of population which is the término-seat

vocal   voting member of a comisión or directiva

Appendix 1
Population Figures
for Almonaster and Selected
Neighboring Términos

The following figures cover the eight términos of Alájar, Almonaster la Real, Aracena, Cortegana, Galaroza, Jabugo, Linares de la Sierra, and Santa Ana la Real. All término-seats are designated as *Villas,* with the exception of Aracena which is designated a city (*ciudad*). Aracena is the capital of the judicial district to which the others also belong. Each término consists of the central town or city and a number of smaller population centers. In addition to aldeas, these may include mines, train stations and industrial centers (all normally designated as *caserios*). Since a small percentage of each término's population lives dispersed throughout the countryside, these persons are included in the totals for the nearest population center. The specific breakdown is only available in the records of each Ayuntamiento and is not presented here.

Two sets of figures are given in Spanish census reports, legal residents (*de derecho*) and the number actually in residence (*de hecho*). In the following charts only the totals of actual residents (*de hecho*) are given.[1] All figures were supplied by the Ayuntamiento of Almonaster la Real.

[1]The difference between these two sets of figures is usually quite small, the *derecho* total being the same as, or a few persons larger than, the *hecho* total. The only major exception to this pattern is in the case of the mines. When a mine is doing well, the *derecho* total may be a good deal smaller than the number of people actually in residence *(de hecho)*; a newly abandoned mine may have just the opposite profile.

Census of 1960 In Residence Population of Eight Términos

Término	1960	1950	Population of Central Town, 1950	Number of Additional Centers	1940	Population of Central Town, 1940	Number of Additional Centers 1940	1930	1920	1910	1900
Alájar	1,540	1,769	1,419	7[a]	1,921	1,501	7[a]	2,131	2,386	2,421	2,491
Almonaster la Real	5,171	4,518	916	25[b]	4,770	865	28[c]	7,973	9,131	8,288	4,182
Aracena	7,643	8,074	5,859	17	7,737	5,668	17	7,320	6,618	6,454	6,281
Cortegana	8,344	7,344	5,086	11	7,179	4,688	13	7,559	6,742	6,313	5,716
Galaroza	2,610	2,553	2,274	2[d]	2,684	2,367	2[d]	2,715	2,821	2,776	2,621
Jabugo	3,376	3,304	1,714	4	3,540	1,842	3[e]	3,230	3,094	2,657	2,397
Linares de la Sierra	601	648	648	0	758	729	3[f]	808	863	813	821
Santa Ana la Real	923	1,018	563	3	1,164	566	3	1,069	910	854	983

[a] plus 2 deserted centers
[b] plus 6 deserted centers
[c] plus 4 deserted centers

[a] plus 1 deserted center
[c] plus 2 deserted centers
[f] plus 2 deserted centers

Twenty-five Year Chart of the Population of the
Término of Almonaster la Real

Population Center	Type	Distance from Central Town in Km.	1940	1950	1965
Acebuches	aldea	4.1	124	155	112
Aguafría	aldea	5.5	173	172	135
Aguas Teñidas	caserío	13	75	75	38
Almonaster	villa	0	865	916	747
Angelita	caserío	11.5	0	NLA[a]	NLA
Arroyo	aldea	3	198	215	203
Calabazares	aldea	4	295	293	180
Canaleja	aldea	3.5	173	185	121
Cincho	aldea	4.5	30	32	13
Concepción	caserío	16	342	116	558
Cueva de la Mora	caserío	11	407	193	346
Dehesa	aldea	10.3	271	239	166
Escalada	aldea	4	165	188	128
Esperanza	caserío	17.3	0	7	3
Estación Almonaster	caserío	4.3	85	92	96
Estación Gil Márquez	caserío	7.5	70	50	22
Gil Márquez	aldea	7.1	184	229	198
Guijo (El)	caserío	18	4	NLA	NLA
Joya (La)	caserío	19	73	98	236
Juliana (La)	aldea	9.4	122	93	48
Lantiseares	caserío	18.1	4	NLA	NLA
Manzano (El)	sulfer spa	6.5	3	4	0
Molares	aldea	3.5	113	154	97
Monte Romero	caserío	11.7	0	NLA	NLA
Patrás	aldea	12	354	362	311
Rincomalillo	aldea	7.7	21	16	30
San Carlos	caserío	4.7	5	NLA	NLA
San Fernando	caserío	11.5	0	NLA	NLA
San Miguel	caserío	14.8	35	65	151
San Platón	caserío	17.5	88	25	15
Serpos	aldea	8	78	76	42
Veredas	aldea	4.5	418	468	414

[a]NLA = No longer appears.

Appendix 2
The Song Types of Almonaster

In the chapters on the festival cycle of Almonaster, songs were presented as part of the data. They were set down without regard for their characteristic vocal forms. Although all songs are four or five lines long in their literary form, there are at least three major forms when sung. These forms depend on the ritual use to which they are put and on the length of the original poem. In the following examples the numbers to the left of the line correspond to the number that line would have in its literary form.

COPLAS DEL ROMERO

These poems are all four lines long. They are only sung during the ritual parades of the festival of the Cross of May. In their vocal form they are always nine lines long.

1 Es tan estrecha la cama
2 donde Jesucristo duerme
2 donde Jesucristo duerme
3 que por no poder estar
4 un pie sobre el otro tiene
4 un pie sobre el otro tiene
4 un pie sobre el otro tiene,
1 Es tan estrecha la cama
2 donde Jesucristo duerme

FANDANGOS DE LA CRUZ

These songs are sung before and after all of the major processions of the Crosses festival and during the preliminary rites. Fandangos are all four or five line poems. The Fandangos of the Cross are all sung as six line songs.

2 de no volverte mirar
1 Al pie de una cruz juré
2 de no volverte mirar.
3 Fué tan grande mi querer
4 que tuve que quebrantar
5 el juramento que eche.

2 quien tiene piña, piñones
1 Alto pino tiene piña,
2 quien tiene piña, piñones;
3 quien tiene amor, tiene celos;
4 quien tiene celos, pasiones.
1 Alto pino tiene piña

1 El fandango es mi alegría,
1 El fandango es mi alegría,
2 el cante que llegue al cielo,
3 que quita las penas mias,
4 un fandanguillo llanero.
1 El fandango es mi alegría

FANDANGOS DE SANTA EULALIA

These songs are sung throughout the festival of Santa Eulalia and during the rest of the year. The poems are all four or five lines long and are always sung as five line songs.

1 Camino de Santa Eulalia
2 una niña se perdió;
3 Virgen de la Candelaria
4 si me la encontrara yo
5 una salve le rezaba.

1 En Santa Eulalia hay un rio
2 que le llaman Sancolí
3 donde me lavé la cara
4 la primera vez que fuí.
1 En Santa Eulalia hay un rio

Professional singers who include Fandangos of Santa Eulalia as part of their repertoire usually sing these songs in a six line form, 212345 or 212341.

SONG DIFFUSION

Although Almuñenses take great pride in having their own fandango style, music, and poetry, as a community hallmark, these elements are certainly part of a broad network which communicates new compositions from one area to the next. Certainly a large number of fandangos are composed every year (especially for Santa Eulalia) by and for Almuñenses, but there is also evidence for diffusion. The following are two traditional songs from Almonaster compared to two recorded by Caro Baroja (1968) from other parts of Huelva.

Viva el Llano que es mi tierra
y San Martín mi patrón.
Viva la gente del Llano,
porque del Llano soy yo.
(Fandango de la Santa Cruz del Llano,
Almonaster la Real)

Viva el Cerro, que es mi tierra;
San Benito mi patrón.
Viva la gente del Cerro,
porque cerreño soy yo.
(Fandango de San Benito, El Cerro de
Andévalo. Baroja 1968:46)[1]

La Virgen de Santa Eulalia
la que más altares tiene;
no hay uno en Almonaster
que en su pecho no la lleve.
(Fandango de Santa Eulalia, Almonaster
la Real)

Es la Virgen de la Peña
la que más altares tiene;
no hay hijo de La Puebla
que en su pecho no la lleve.
(Fandango de Neustra Señora de la Peña,
Puebla de Guzmán. Baroja 1968:35)[1]

[1]From *Estudios Sobre La Vida Tradicional Española* by Julio Caro Baroja. Copyright© 1968. Reprinted by permission of Edicions 62 S/A, Publishers.

Appendix 3
The Ritual Calendar of
Almonaster and Selected Aldea

The following chart gives the major holiday festivals and rituals in Almonaster and some of the larger aldeas and mines. The dates are from the year 1968.

Jan. 6   Day of the Three Kings—festival in Veredas.
Feb. 25   Carnivál—Baile Disfraz in Almonaster (costume dance)
April 7-14   Semana Santa—processions in Almonaster
May 3   Invention of the Cross—festivals in Veredas and Aguafría
May 4-8   Crosses of May festival in Almonaster
May 17-19   Romería of Santa Eulalia
June 13   Corpus Cristi
June 20-22   Festivities in Acebuches
June 22-23   Festival of San Juan Bautista in Monte Blanco
June 24   Block party for San Juan Bautista in Almonaster
July 29   Block party for Saints Pedro y Pablo in Almonaster
July 16-17   Festival of Nuestra Señora del Carmen in Gil Márquez
July 17-20   Secular festivities in Cueva de la Mora mine
July 25   Festival of Santiago Apóstol in Arroyo
July 27-28   Festival of Sagrado Corazón de Jesús in La Canaleja
Aug. 2-3   Festival of Virgen de Fátima in Calabazares
Aug. 10   Festival in Los Romeros
Aug. 11   Festival of Nuestra Señora de Fátima in Veredas
Aug. 15   Holiday of La Asunción—Secular festival in Almonaster

Aug. 17   Festival of the Virgen de la Asunción in Escalada
Aug. 17   Festival at Valdelamusa mine
Aug. 24-26   Feria in Almonaster, Nuestra Señora del Dolores
Aug. 31-Sept. 3   Festival of Virgen del Rosario in Patrás
Oct. 27   Festival of Cristo Rey in Aguafría
Nov. 20   National holiday of José Antonia Primo de Rivera
Dec. 25   Noche Buena
Dec. 31   Noche Vieja

Appendix 4
Rough Statistics
on Multicommunity
Exogamy/Endogamy

In the case of Almonaster and seven aldeas, enough life history material was available to construct rough measures of exogamy/endogamy. This was done after the period of field research and is plagued by as yet unanswerable questions. The method was to tabulate the number of marriage pairs within the community. Three separate totals were obtained: (1) the sum of all marriages with one or both spouses originating in the multicommunity [total pairs]; (2) the sum of all marriages with one spouse from outside the multicommunity [exogamous pairs]; (3) the sum of all marriages in which both spouses originated outside the multicommunity [exogamous squared pairs]. This third exogamous squared figure was not included in the "total pairs" figure and is only included for comparison with the other raw data. The measure of exogamy is expressed as the percentage of the sum of the total pairs represented by the exogamous pairs.

Marriages in which one of the spouses was deceased were included if the provenience of the dead spouse was known. Because of insufficient data, it was not possible to measure exogamy/endogamy between communities of the same multicommunity; rather each measure for a specific community is expressed with relation to the outside of the multicommunity. It remains for the future to construct measures of the extent to which individual communities are exogamous/endogamous within the context of the multicommunity.

Acebuches   (exogamous pairs) 7 ÷ (total pairs) 37 = 18.9% exogamous
   Exogamous^2 pairs = 1 (not included in total pairs)
Arroya   (exo. pairs) 7 ÷ (total pairs) 55 = 12.7% exogamous
   Exo.^{2} pairs = 3 (not included in total pairs)
Calabazares   (exo. pairs) 10 ÷ (total pairs) 68 = 14.7% exogamous
   Exo.^{2} pairs = 0
Escalada   (exo. pairs) 5 ÷ (total pairs) 38 = 13.2% exogamous
   Exo.^{2} pairs = 1 (not included in total pairs)
Gil Márquez   (exo. pairs) 12 ÷ (total pairs) 47 = 25.5% exogamous
   Exo.^{2} pairs = 1 (not included in total pairs)
Molares   (exo. pairs) 5 ÷ (total pairs) 29 = 17.2% exogamous
   Exo.^{2} pairs = 0
Veredas   (exo. pairs) 7 ÷ (total pairs) 130 = 5.4% exogamous
   Exo.^{2} pairs = 0

ALMONASTER BY ECONOMIC CATEGORIES

A)   Retired workers, agricultural workers, industrial and construction workers.
     (exo. pairs) 27 ÷ (total pairs) 105 = 25.7% exogamous
     Exo.^{2} pairs = 4 (not included in total pairs)

B)   Businessmen, professionals, specialists, government employees, government pensioners.
     (exo. pairs) 18 ÷ (total pairs) 73 = 24.7% exogamous
     Exo.^{2} pairs = 10 (not included in total pairs)

C)   Small and middle cash farmers.
     (exo. pairs) 0 ÷ (total pairs) 12 = 0% exogamous
     Exo.^{2} pairs = 0

D)   Large landowners.
     (exo. pairs) 12 ÷ (total pairs) 21 = 57.1% exogamous
     Exo.^{2} pairs = 0

A number of causal factors are indicated, but too little data is available to do more than indicate a few of them. Geography, lines of communication and land resources are implied in almost every case. For example, Gil Márquez, with 25.5% exogamy, is on the railroad line and has its own station. Veredas (5.4% exogamy) is under intensive agriculture with one of the largest numbers of middle-sized cash farmers outside of Almonaster itself.

In all the aldeas, inter-community marriages are common but do not appear in these statistics, though this fact accounts in part for their low exogamy percentages.

Bibliography

Aguilera, Francisco E.
    1972   Santa Eulalia's People: The Anatomy of an Andalucian Multicommunity. Ph. D. dissertation, Anthropology Department, University of Pennsylvania.
    1976   Changes in Economic Strategy: Secularization of "Peasants" or Normal Community Process? *In* Economic Transformation and Steady State Values. J. B. Aceves, E. C. Hansen, and G. Levitas, eds. Queens College Publications in Anthropology, Number 2. Pp. 30–41. Flushing, NY: Queens College Press.

Arensberg, Conrad M.
    1961   The Community as Object and as Sample. American Anthropologist 63:241–264.

Arsobispado de Sevilla
    1791   Plan y decreto de erección y dotación de curatos del Arsobispado de Savilla, Año 1791. Sevilla.

Bateson, Gregory.
    1958   Naven. 2d ed. Stanford: Stanford University Press.

Caro Baroja, Julio
    1957   El sociocentirismo de los pueblos españoles. *In* Razas, pueblos y linajes. Madrid: Revista de Occidente.
    1968   Estudios Sobre La Vida Tradicional Española. Barcelona: Ediciones Península.

Fortes, Meyer
    1953   The Structure of Unilineal Descent Groups. American Anthropologist 55:17–41. *In* Cultures and Societies of Africa. Simon and Phoebe Ottenberg, eds. Pp. 163–188. New York: Random House.

Freeman, Susan T.
    1968   Corporate Village Organization in the Sierra Ministra: An Iberian
            Structural Type. Man, n.s. 3:477–484.

Friedl, Ernestine
    1968   Book review of *Culture and Community* by Arensberg and Kimball.
            American Anthropologist 68:1022–1024.

Masegui
    1969   Las Cruces de Bonares y su Romerito. Huelva: Odiel May 10:4.

Montero Escalera, Francisco
    1967   Fandangos de Santa Eulalia. Almonaster la Real: privately published.

Murdock, George Peter
    1949   Social Structure. New York: Macmillan.

Ottenberg, Simon, and Phoebe Ottenberg, eds.
    1960   Cultures and Societies of Africa. New York: Random House.

Peristiany, J. G., ed.
    1966   Honor and Shame. Chicago: University of Chicago Press.

Pitt-Rivers, Julian A.
    1961   The People of the Sierra. Chicago: University of Chicago Press.

Reina, Rubén E.
    1965   Town, Community and Multicommunity. Estudios de Cultura Maya
            5:361–390.

Ayuntamiento de Almonaster La Real (Huelva)
            Various census records through 1966–1967.

Wagley, Charles, and Marvin Harris
    1955   A Typology of Latin American Subcultures. American Anthropolo-
            gist 57:428–451.

Wallace, Anthony F. C.
    1956   Revitalization Movements. American Anthropologist 58:264–281.

Wolf, Eric R.
    1955   Types of Latin American Peasantries: A Preliminary Discussion.
            American Anthropologist 57:452–471.

Index

†